CRICKET COUNTRY

CRICKET COUNTRY

EDMUND BLUNDEN

THE IMPRINT SOCIETY

LONDON

THIS EDITION PUBLISHED BY THE REPRINT SOCIETY LTD.
BY ARRANGEMENT WITH WM. COLLINS SONS AND CO. LTD.
1945

TO

F. W. WAGNER

IN GRATITUDE FOR OUR

MANY TALKS

PRINTED IN GREAT BRITAIN
BY COLLINS CLEAR-TYPE PRESS: LONDON AND GLASGOW

Preface

ONE MORNING before the world was again at war I received the following verses, which had been composed in allusion to some of my own of still more distant date:

> Have you not ever felt the urge to write
> Of all the cricket that has blessed your sight?
> Is there no inspiration in the names
> Of those that play our best of summer games?
> You, to whom every detail must be dear,
> And every subtlety and beauty clear:
> The deep content of cricket in the sun,
> The æsthete's pleasure, and the batsman's fun,
> And under driving clouds, the greatest day
> When battle's waged and bowlers have their way—
> Even the dullest grey day's bitter chill
> Without the haze of glory's cricket still,
> Cricket in every mood, leisure of soul,
> Basking or shivering, to enjoy the whole. . . .

I was delighted with these lines, and yet the challenge which they delivered was formidable. My poet proceeded:

> If actual play is not enough for rhyme,
> These are the moods that linger on in time:
> Autumn, fresh summer visions in the mind,
> Created from a season left behind ;
> Winter, the sudden need to talk to those
> Who number football among cricket's foes;
> Spring, in the sun, quickening intense the pain
> Of too soon feeling summer come again;
> Then summer, wet or fine, and cricket's there,
> A day's reality for dreams in air. . . .

And there was this generous remonstrance as the conclusion of Cordelia's message:

> The summer evening sound of bat and ball
> Haunts through your verse—but is that to be all?
> You "seek and serve a beauty that must die"—
> Must cricket's beauty then unwritten lie?
> Cricket should dare you take your pen and write
> "Worthy the reading and the world's delight."
> Dare you among your writings leave but one
> Of this your "worship in the summer sun"?

The poem so gracefully flattering to an author whose friendships and habits had certainly kept him in touch with its subject was not forgotten. But no practical response could be made to my kind enthusiast before the new war broke with its overwhelming shadows upon our world. Then, of course, there was no thinking of the old serene enjoyments and their essence and worth for year upon year. But at length the burden began to shift from our minds, not because the war was as good as over—I wish it were; but because the fuller procession of time and mankind in his many activities and expressions became clearer through the rage of the present strife, as that could be seen in proportion. It chanced while this feeling was reviving round me that my friend Milton Waldman encouraged me by desiring, much as my poetical cricketer had done, that I would write a book with the cricket field as its central cone, or seed-plot. And here, however it comes out now that it is done, the book is offered.

In writing it I have regarded myself as given a roving commission; and the subject itself would have defied any rigid scheme of composition. But I venture to hope that I have followed a continuous, even if a winding and sometimes tangled path. I have been told of an eighteenth-century novel which begins more or less with the lobbing of a cricket ball by young squire Orlando through the open window where his adored Monimia is sitting; the ball bounces against a family portrait (Sir Hildebrand on his white horse whose flanks are overshadowed by his stupendous wig); Monimia neatly flicks the ball under the chairs, but her dragon aunt has more than a little suspicion of what is going on, and—so the story gets moving. Monimia is forbidden to speak to Orlando, but at the end of the fourth volume this cricketer gets her, and Rayland Hall. Maybe this briefer essay of mine has gone on its way in the same sort of free but not uncontrolled progress.

Should it be found to suffer from moments of inconsequential movement, I can only wish that they may bear the redeeming unconscious charm of a non-sequitur which among others rewarded me lately for a toilsome journey through an old autobiography: "My boy-companions, of a year or two older, were continually going to sea with the white collar, dirk at the side, changing school restraint for real danger. One of them, stationed in the tops, struck by a chain-shot, fell on the deck, in halves, on his first cruise. Provisions were scarce at the time."

I must conclude, and in conclusion I cannot but touch on a different note. Since *Cricket Country* was finished in manuscript, we have read in our newspapers with great grief that a player whose genius and character had long been the admiration of the cricket world has died of wounds received in battle. Captain Hedley Verity is numbered now among those wonderful cricketers whom we never dreamed of losing except by the normal action of time and retirement, and whose memory will be honoured as well for their promptitude, their ability and their bravery when war confronted them with its new and violent problems. Verity's tall and well-poised figure, his entire expression of accurate strategy arranging all the game to his intention save for his respect for the other arrangers, his trust in the fine art of his cricket no matter how much some crashing interlude of sheer shock tactics seemed to disqualify it, will stay with us who saw him in his decorous triumphs. In thinking of him and the others who have gone from cricket with the honours of the fighting man fallen in action, I am reassured over the little book that I have written—at least, about the cause which I think it and others like it may serve. If it should help in its degree to disclose the secret of the cricket world in which such men found and gave happiness, and so be a memorial to their excellence and that which they understood so well, it needs no apology however serious its defects and its errors may be.

E. B.

September, 1943.

Contents

The Native Heath

BESIDE that small round pond which is almost kept a secret by the massed spears of reeds rank upon rank, and beside the casual thistle-topped track which leads to an out-post farm in a kind of Netherlandish country of dikes and pollards and people working on stilts, nobody would expect to see a game of cricket played. Perhaps none ever is now. The house hard by with roofs like cliffs is in the possession of strangers, and the woods which once grew primroses enough for all the children for miles to gather and then no lack, scarcely know the flower. But in the thistly field by the pond I can remember more than one game of cricket— I speak of almost forty years ago—as an annual event which has remained in my mind much as though I had been present at some Elizabethan feast of sheep-shearers or haymakers. These old-fashioned games, which nothing of Elizabethan colour or music befriended, happened once a year, well before the general season of cricket began, and without any selection committees or posted notices. The word would go round among the boys that, however marvellous it sounded while spring was still doubtfully contesting "unmatured green vallies cold," the match in the meadow by the pond would be played on the approaching holiday.

So on the day we went. "Way up, Noble." "What cheer, Goog." There was no question of choosing the players, or eleven a side. Those who came, played. They were of all sizes, little chaps and big; in all costumes, some in loose black leggings, some with trousers tied below the knee with coconut twine; and no particular sides were picked up. So long as someone was bowling, someone batting, the rest fielding out (with varying enthusiasm), and everybody umpir-

ing, the match was always a success. It faded away without
the strife of aggregates. The players were chiefly unfamiliar
faces to me, for this field lay at the end of our sprawling
parish, and the sportsmen came together from secluded
cottages far down lanes bordering the orchards and shaws
and hop-gardens thereabouts. What continued to keep me
thinking was by no means the performance with bat and
ball, a whiskery old ball, but the odd spontaneity of the
whole assembly, once a year; and I observed that the young
men, and one or two watch-chained elders, who then
appeared as cricketers, did not for the most part make
another appearance in this line of business when summer
offered full chances. Indeed, even to my childish eye, they
cut rather awkward figures in such appearances. What made
them risk 'it, this once a year? What old tradition of
crowded games and dances had dwindled into this pathetic
little outing?

The thing might have stayed in my thoughts just as an
isolated antiquarian trifle; yet, when time had carried me
beyond that extreme boundary of my old home, making
things once habitual claim the right of the peculiar and
significant, I was more and more impressed by the depth of
the cricket tradition in that part of England. It arose like a
ghost out of the ground, haunting this or that stretch of
short grass or pathway side, luring us to it without question
or anything but willing hearts. On occasion (in the true
ghost way) the spirit was absent, and though the fine evening
would seem the most gloriously suitable for the game, nobody turned up. Probably garden or farm jobs prevailed.
These intervals did no harm to the next occasions when once
more plenty of us came along to the unmarked place of play,
and kept up an eager contest till the livelong daylight had
failed and there was only glimmer enough for jests and
pranks. I could draw a map of the several cricket pitches
which nature and custom got ready for us, between the
immemorial ring of trees by the weir where the past had
seen celebrated cricketers flourish, and the mill-pool two

miles east, by the banks of which pleasant-voiced Mrs. Bellamy used to bowl a brilliantly varnished bouncing ball with pictures on it at her young family and their friends. It would be a map of something more than a child's play, if there is much more in human life than that.

Digressions may multiply in these pages, and this point may be almost too early for one; but as I think of those games, coming and going like wild flowers, a short speech from one of my first companions is distinct in my hearing. It will be a clearer comment than anything of my own. The cottage gardeners' flower-show of every summer was regularly the occasion for a game among the boys of the National School, who pitched their brass-topped stumps excitedly in the corner of the flaring meadow—the roundabouts would do later in the day, *and* the coconuts. My father joined in, and accordingly the cricket gained dignity and, for an hour or so, was as monotonous to us as a Test Match. There he stood at the wicket on one afternoon never to be forgotten —a batsman of some calibre, a grown-up, a large batsman. Behind the other wicket Will Bellamy, who was a sturdy boy, with a mighty serious expression, clutching the ball in one hand and clenching the other, prepared to bowl at the giant. The first or second time he tried the ball sailed over an oak tree in the next meadow, aromatic with swathes of new-mown hay. Once or twice more the ball flew afar as the magician smote. But then, not quite losing hope, Will whirled his arm over again, the bat flashed and the wicket fell! I am not sure that the game was allowed to continue after this climax; but I recollect (when time had travelled on) walking past the empty field under the starry arch of a December night with Will, who, being about twelve years of age, crowned a solemn conversation with the following pronouncement: "I think that was the Best Ball I ever Bowled *in my life.*"

The tradition of the game in our valley of the orchards maintaining its easy succession year upon year, suddenly grew clearer to me a long time afterwards on an evening when, sitting at a window overlooking the green and listening to the shouts of "Throw in" caused by the slashing batsmanship of a black-haired girl there, I glanced into the newly bought volume of letters of an eighteenth-century poet. The popular author of *The Minstrel* (as I then discovered) stayed now and then in a mood of Arcadian fondness and the picturesque, in the village adjoining ours. He was a Scot, but was not unkind to our southern manners, and he did not disdain to record in his reports to the philosophers at home a cricket match of yearly consequence played, with lots of beer and cheerfulness, in a field opposite the village church. There amid the long grass matches were still being played until the first World War, and may yet be after the second, though Sports Clubs perhaps do not quite pass as direct heirs of the sons of the village, in sight of their friend and enemy the "stubborn glebe," taking off their jackets as if to assail it once again—but this time for a diversion.

Long live diversion! Among all the charming things that I have had the luck to meet with in town and country, the unofficial, undeveloped game and play will not swiftly lose my love, even though I may not now or ever delve out my reason for loving it. Yet many others besides must feel a lightening of all that was a burden when all of a sudden the children, punctual as the swallow or the bluebell, and inquiring no more than those into the theory of their revivals, come out with the sport of the season. Wanton wits inform me that these seasons of games are directed by nothing more mysterious than business ingenuity; but I cannot see that at the present hour when the little boys are lashing far from new tops, and not less fascinated than in better times, when new tops were so numerous. Marbles, tops of various shape and various function—the window-breaker never was so bad as his name, the peg-top always looked more sinister to me—had-you-last, tipcat or nipcat, rounders, skipping, hopscotch, high-cockalorum, wagon and horses, show-your-light, hide-ee-up, hoops, sheep and wolf and a host of other sports besides cricket with a rag ball, come kindly out of the past at childhood's call. When it is decided that the new one must come, the old goes away in a twinkling into the strange country where it sleeps. Some of these games, you may tell me, are under suspicion of having gone for ever,—

"Where's Troy, and where's the Maypole in the Strand?"

Modernity does not refrain from the toys of children; games in the end must die like parts of Homer and Shakespeare, or be modified as much as the cricket bat of to-day, spliced and complex-handled, is altered from the curved cudgel of the same name in the days of George the Third. Modification is a deity worth a canto of some new poet's imagining. When we reflect that, as a masterly philologer was reminding me lately, "a newt" and "an eft" are the same word, we may conclude that the unusual appearance of a thing does not constitute a new thing. Because we did not lately see a game we knew, a toy we smiled at in the village street or in Mariners' Court, we need not at once turn to composing elegies for its being at last irrecoverably sent away from the world. The game may, like baseball, subject to this modification, rise afresh in a shape of rapid tremendous power, conquering continents. Or it may steal in among its old company very much as it was, a *revenant* which frightens nobody and in action is as courteous and acceptable as the weather around its glittering eyes and clapping hands.

I sometimes hear it proposed that cricket, the ever changeful, changeless game which some even among the English view as the prime English eccentricity, is a something to which, for thorough appreciation, a man must have been bred from the cradle [1] or about there. If this is the truth, I qualify; for in our village and our county the game was so native, so constant, so beloved without fuss that it came to me as the air I breathed and the morning and evening.

---

[1] The old story is not so well known now as to be withheld: A member of a noted cricketing family was asked what he thought of the promise of a younger brother. He answered, "Not much; but he's had no chance, poor fellow, he was too delicate to begin till he was SIX years old."

Time has altered me, though some who know me will not admit it in this connection; but there were many of us whose childhood was moulded in the same way. Some boys of course did not enjoy cricket, and we wondered at them, and thought them unsocial. Some of the older people reproved the zealous as "cricket-mad," but we heard that for all their growlings they were once players—indeed it came out that Mr. J. who frowned and even cast imprecations on the noise of our playground game, was a collector of books on cricket. Others never took a seat on the boundary of the village ground, who all the same did not miss a football match. Still, it may be held that cricket lay much as Wordsworth's heaven about boys like me in our infancy, in act and word colouring our minds—and who was I to quarrel with the world into which I had come? There perpetually you had the cherry orchard, there the grammar school, there the dairy farm, the brewery, the wharf, the church, the cricket field—and I was convinced, if convincing was required, that God had been doing his best in all these arrangements.

Those were the days of clergymen cricketers. Our own vicar was the greatest example of these whom I ever saw. I have certainly encountered others whose careers were longer—one, for example, who delivered at me the most agitating underhand bowling at the age of seventy, and duly added me to his monotonous list of victims. But the impression this ancient lobster made was in every way narrower. It astonished me to watch the vicar on Sundays in summer, when morning and evening for a few hours he became the priest and bore the sway and dignity, imparted the light and consolation of a sound divine. I secretly marvelled that this should be the same man who yesterday kept wicket and slaughtered the over-pitched ball with such absolute, single devotion. It was a similar though a lowlier Sabbath mystery in the case of some of the choirmen, who had divested themselves, it seemed, not only of their cricket boots and pads but also of their principal object in life—for that one day of the week. But I had my suspicions. In the vestry, during the crowded expectant moments before we marched forth singing our hymn, or "Lead me, Lord" to our choir seats, I observed that the vicar with a rich smile would sometimes hold a whispered conversation apart with one or two of his cricketers. It might have been, of course, enlightenment on a theological nicety, or a thought on church music, but I did get the impression that the Sunday paper had not been safely received at the Vicarage before the vicar left, and that some such inquiry as "How many did Kent make altogether?" or "Did the Australians put us in, then?" was made and answered. (News in those days did not come before its time.) Or it might be something nearer home: "That fellow you ran out seemed pretty miserable about something, Judd."—"Yes, sir, he told the scorer that you had told him to go—' safe run there, my boy.'"—"Well, —did I?" stroking a smooth chin as if in a deep considera- tion.[1]

The epitaph of the vicar now glimmers upon the nave of the church which he, so many years, served with ability, affection and religion. It is a just tribute to his worth as a parish priest, though no short inscription could intimate that handsome presence (yielding a touch of the Falstaffian peculiarly blended with the aristocratic) or renew the strong and stirring notes of that voice. "When the wicked man turneth away from his wickedness. . . ." "Let your light so shine before men" (how welcome he made the very offer- tory!)—monitions like these echo on for me still in his intonation, and even as a child I determined that, as *he* had drawn my attention to them, I ought to do something about them. He, if any one in the land, had authority. The tablet to his memory cannot re-create the light of his coun- tenance, though it gives his dates; and in the opinion of some who knew him it lacks something else, which was not beyond its powers or its proper nature. The centuries will

---

[1] "Id, quod fieri non debet, factum valet," but I don't think the vicar had any legal training.

read it (if the bombs go on missing it, as a scattering of them did one startling summer night) never guessing that the subject was for many summers the pattern of cricket enthusiasm, the incumbent of the village ground. And in that era that was something.

Biographical information on any man's gravestone has been growing sparser lately than I could wish. I have a passion for it. I love to be allowed a little more to see of the men and women who once enjoyed life, or experienced it at least, than bare names and chronology allow. It may be nothing to them, as Thomas Hardy felt when he wrote the wonderful elegiac song, "Friends Beyond," but it is something to us who can still consider "the moral and the mystery of man." Somewhere I read the last letter of a man who was about to be hanged for a murder, and as I remember it, it bore a postscript, "No more cricket, George." If that were added to any inscription which indicated the other part of the story, it might be a voice from the tomb which would not require the old preamble, "Stop, passer-by."

Our cordial parson, to come back to the upper side of the daisies, was well known in many a cricket field besides our own, and in higher company than our local matches attracted; sometimes, it may be, he put over an old sermon because the week's demands on him and his cricket bag had given no time for writing a new one. ("How did you like my sermon?" "I like it better every time I hear it.") I only know of one cricketer who could combine the most able attention to a terrific match with the writing of something as remote from it as the works of Sir Thomas Browne. It was not our old friend. He put on his white sun-hat with a single purpose, a first great Cause. The vicar was a wicket-keeper of heavy build but a light and menacing rapidity in action. As has been hinted, he did not spare the foolish, and they say he played some tricks on his slower-thinking adversaries. I saw him once stump a batsman with such utter speed and indolence mixed as Ames of Kent in later days could show when Freeman lured the striker out of his ground—but the vicar's chance on the occasion I noted was the briefest imaginable. When his turn came to swing the bat he attacked the ball with a vengeance other than the Lord's, but possibly a theologian could explicate a relationship and justify the vicar's own Article. A slovenly bad ball, "a godly and wholesome doctrine" of driving it and all such out of the earth.

As he grew old, and fell lame, the world underwent changes which he did not find easy—who did? There was a local change which must often have grieved him when he looked forth from the fine vicarage windows southward, into that lustrous light which is so often found over the valley there. The cricket ground, scene of so many of his deeds and quips and social interchanges, had been ploughed up during the first World War, and was no longer used except by fat sheep cleaning up kale. The velvety greensward, the music of the bat well used, the laugh at the unfortunate "leatherhunter" on a hot chase, the bearded mower going to and from behind the horse in his leather shoes, the old men commending or disrelishing play from the bench by the oak, the call from the pavilion that sent the tins hustling up on the scoreboard, the players arriving with their radiant caps and blazers, or strolling out to the pitch with bare heads catching the sunlight, the deck chairs, the teacups, the gentle ladies who presided over them—none there any more. Just stripped, untidy stems of kale.

Yet the old man would have himself driven down to the new ground, though it was not the rendezvous for all the old schools and all the lions of polite cricket that the old one had been. Sitting forward in the pavilion (*that* structure at least had survived and had made itself at home in a new situation) he scanned the match with a quiet eye, and he seemed to approve of what he saw. At last he fell talking very gently (we had heard him in other voice) of things long past, and he did not lack a hearer or two who could travel back over that road with him, a little surprised to find it so. He talked, as old people are said to do so much, of small matters that had chanced long before and might have been supposed to have left no mark as they flitted by; but we see that it is the great ones which may pass more utterly. His memories arose in multitude as he sat composedly there, cricket coincidence, humours, personal touches among them but not only those; for he had discerned that the game itself, if it is found in its natural bearings, is only the agreeable wicket-gate to a landscape of human joys and sorrows, and is greatest where it fades away most imperceptibly into their wider horizon. Glance from your post in the long field, young cricketer (the next batsman is taking his full two minutes to come in) away to those farms and woods, spires and hills about you; rest your high spirits a moment on the composure of that young mother with her sleeping baby, on the old white horse as still as if he was carved in chalk on the down. One day you will seek in your mind for the scores of the match which are now so important and definite, and they will not be there—only, in place of them, the assurance of an eternal summer, a grace that homes within the minds and hearts of your kindred, and around all their works and days.

We knew more than one young cricketer for whom the favourite game darkened into a premature sunless season. No one was ever spoken of more kindly by everybody, nor perhaps with higher or oftener repeated hopes, so far as a village view extends. Freddie, or Froggie, was a born athlete, and upon a scene where most plodded on with mere rustic sturdiness he arrived with the economy and roguery of the artist. He was a little fellow, and a shapely one, like the poet Keats; and he had a face eloquent of strength and intention like the poet Keats, as I may say now that I have become familiar with that occasional cricketer's portraits. A good style of speech and selection of knowledge distinguished him, he could play a bugle and he could sing, he did all with a charming attentiveness to the instructor; but his country fame was drawn from football and even more

from cricket. When it was my honour, and immense it was
that day, to play in a match for the first time, I was sent
creeping in to bat at the end of an innings, and the other
batsman was Fred, who had been in possession of the wicket
for an hour or more. His score was sixty so far, and he had
been breaking all the rules of academic batsmanship to
everybody's satisfaction. By the kindness of all concerned I
was not prevented from holding up one end until, with ever
increasing glorious freedom, he had achieved what was then
almost a mythical feat—his hundred runs.

To me, on whom reflected glory beamed for a minute,
when that day was becoming distant, the hero still appeared
almost literally "apparelled in celestial light." He went on
his way, in the cricket of the region, on our own ground or
on others (the torment of missing him!) and all the way
his brilliance grew. Clubs flourishing in places miles off
tempted him to play for them, and not just for the runs he
brought them. I still remember a discussion among my
elders of some enchanting innings by him which brought
quite a modest total in runs.

One day I saw him at the church steps, with a flushed
face, a bright colouring of which I was not old enough to
understand the omen until someone told me. He was going
to die. Still I hoped, and the next time I saw him, languid in
a wheeled chair, I asked him when he would have another
last-wicket partnership with me. He could smile at that;
but his cricket had already gone dim while, as I heard in
scraps of talk, he religiously contemplated the world to
which he was going. "Going home," the farm labourers
called it. How quietly he was going! In the vast and
bewildering music of the world I have known, to this hour
his song is clear, now so quick and lyrical, and then so slow
and petitioning. Perhaps it amounts to that ancient one
after all, "Whom the Gods love, die young."

The village is not small, in extent or population, and in
the old vicar's reign it had a first and a second cricket team;
so far as I could judge such matters these were divided quite

firmly by the barrier of class. It was only now and then that one of the villagers proper, such as my beloved Froggie, through sheer accomplishment or upon an unforeseen vacancy, was seen among the grand folks composing the first team. The demands of the workman's week, after all, conflicted with the ample time-table of that polished cricket and that lovely lunch, which was not neglected on account of any state of the game, and yet lovelier tea, from which the ladies soon distributed lots of cream horns and slabs of Madeira cake among the delighted if slightly awestricken little boys round the scoreboard. So the first team was in a sort a minor Marylebone Cricket Club and its players were assembled from near and far. Among these visitants I had more than one hero, not, of course, so dear to my heart as Froggie; but still my heart leapt up at a noonday sight of them on the path to the ground in its best array, like a billiard table but better. Who could have dreamed that the golden-headed, rosy-cheeked young man, the Etonian of the Victorian novelist, whose slow bowling to watch was like a classical deity's physical exercises, should have had almost as brief a career as my young friend? As I trotted with consciousness of my daring beside his long stride, he presently noticed that I was there, and he talked to me—an honour which still retains its flash of sunshine. But he was intent on his cricket, and rescuing his bag from me and giving me a whole sixpence he was soon being slapped on the back in the pavilion, where it was not for me to follow him even if I had had time from school. This tall landowner, and fine, thinking bowler in the Kentish school of slow bowling, measured to an inch of length and almost of break, never came back from the War of 1914-1918 which even he in his higher sphere had been no better able than we to see gathering its fire-hearted tempest over our southern hills.

To follow the fortunes of the first team even when the match was played at home was too difficult for us unless a holiday coincided, and matches played away were only items in the news and appeared in the *Messenger*; or perhaps my father had been summoned (by the vicar, very secret and urgent) from coloured chalks, desk and harmonium to fill the place of the slow bowler. In that case, the day was long; I would fidget about into the last light of evening for his return and report. He had to be coaxed, even then; he was a miserly, disappointing reporter. Had I been looking on, I believe I could have said more by way of description. But he was a cricketer of a devoted nature. I fear he used to bowl with a tense, total mind, and would not then have perceived that the game was leaving him a memory of other things. He did not even, at that date, mention the sublime pies which used to crown one particular cricket lunch table. He does now, *regnante Woolton*; it is worth coupons hearing him!

Altogether, the second eleven was the one for me. For one thing, the players were almost entirely our own, the same men as I saw spraying apple-trees or graining inn parlour doors or fixing taps ; among whom even the clerk from the railway station, which was a little out of the way from the village street, was something of a guest. For another, the games were half-day games and played on Saturdays mostly, and even if they were played "away," the enemy ground was usually not beyond walking distance. Or one might be given a ride in the horse brake, and that meant "good talk" and temporary intimacy with the heroes. They would treat us, could you believe it ! as cricketers, too. "Where's that damned scorebook you boys keep?" grunted Jack Clarke to me—Jack was a figure almost as famous as his friend Froggie—as the wheels clattered over the road to some village beyond the hill. I had it in my pocket, as certainly as a soldier has his paybook, and Jack put on a solemn expression and imaginary spectacles as he looked at the pages, carefully filled. "Who's this that made 90?" he asked. This happened to be my score, but I had to confess that so imposing a figure was reached by adding up a number of very small ones, several weeks' work, I fear. "Well," he said, closing the book and eyeing the country, "I'm disappointed," but he had done his good deed; that little black book had been transformed into more than our private record.

The words of older people, which are little or nothing to them, in the uttering, are often curiously cherished by children. My sisters used to dog the footsteps of the Builder and Contractor, good solid unhurrying steps they were, until he would *say* something. It was sure to be something really good-humoured, and might be followed by the bestowing of a penny, but the conversation was the main adventure, not the cash. These older people knew things. They had a bigger map of possibilities in their minds. They could so nonchalantly open gates and doors, real or thinking ones, which without them would have been locked to us. And they took an interest in *us*—"what standard" we were in, had we spilt the milkcan again since last time, who had the prettiest curls, did we like holidays or the Band of Hope, where was master Gilbert and the rest. The words used by these fathers of mankind were not infrequently attractive in themselves. "How will you do it? Elbow-grease. What's that? You go and try." "Bless me, lost another ball? You want the dibs —the spondulicks—the wherewithal, that's all you want." "He's a *comical* young beggar,"—how right, how unforeknown that adjective was; the problem settled. "I'd say June-eatings was the nicest apple," "Now you ask your good mother to give you some camomile tea next time"—these things were such discoveries. I am sorry "camomile" in our place was now "cow-mumble" as in some, but "mush-a-rooms" was usual. And one day Mr. Ladder would be giving us a wonderful red-handkerchief-full of those.

II

A Fairly Passive Resister

SINCE I have been reconsidering how true-born, indigenous and accepted the game of cricket appeared to be in the days and places which found me most open to the receipt of impressions, fair play requires that I should not conceal a discovery which at the time felt curious. "In the height of my career," I found that not everybody worshipped this sport, or indeed counted it as one of the chief nourishers in life's feast. Nowadays, it is scarcely necessary to say, destructive notices of cricket come to my eye in book after book of candid reminiscence and to my ear in many a conversation. Only a night or two ago a scientist whose work is influencing the course of this war found time from an arm-chair to analyse cricket for me, with his most detached powers. It was observable that he owned as many anecdotes about Dr. Grace as most of us; but I admit that his analysis was headed without ornament "It's a bad game." He compared it ruthlessly from the point of view of its players' chances of being actively employed and unemployed with other games; and in fact I was not able to hold the fort. Still, being no scientist, I shall go ahead. After all, it is a great while now since I was first made aware of the moral and intellectual opposition to what I had taken to be a glory without an enemy in the world.

Of course there were erratic men whom I met in my travels and who never looked like cricket fans even to me. Old Gideon Wooll, an itinerant preacher, who seemed to lead a kind of frog-like life in the swampy woodsides, might be seen with a contraption in his hand for taking pike in ponds without a rod, but that was the nearest he got to cheerfulness. The inquiry, "Playing for Marden Saturday,

Mr. Wooll?" did not even get an answer, as he went on his way with his bag of tracts. Against this view of the religious man, I could set my acquaintance with two summer visitors with north-country accents who came over to talk to a few of us with our "match" in progress. They began with some allusions to redemption, and they gave us some illustrated short stories which they promised would lead to that result, but their next move was to remove their jackets and plant themselves as bowlers at both ends. Their deliveries were very amiable and I was able to get one longish innings. "We shall call you George Hirst," one of them said; but this deceiver, when I returned to the bat later, promptly bowled me out with a sneak and said in orotund satisfaction, "I saw him go first ball—I saw George Hirst go." After this I particularly distrusted his tracts.

There was Mr. Bevil Barnes, an eminent shopkeeper, a tall, attractive, spirited young man—and I discerned that *he* was indifferent to this cricket business, though friendly to a boys' band. There was Monty Jackson, with his William Hazlitt-like face deep in æsthetic meditations; finding that these did not include the latest scores or anything similar, I indulged in impertinences to him, for which he chased me and struck me on the ear in a wholly unæsthetic manner. And this was in the churchyard where peace and quiet ruled. But (not to pursue the matter all round the parish) Anti-Cricket came to be all embodied in One Man, if I may use an expression which has lately had a certain vogue in wider reference. This man, to whose charge I was committed and to whom I shall never be ungrateful, then represented for me the highest exercises of the mind, the dominions of Erasmus.

Daily in his majesty he strode into our midst, doors banging behind him, in inseparable mortar-board and rusty scholar's gown, adjusting the poise of the one and smoothing down the pennants of the other as he ritually extracted a small length of cane from his black desk. His "Good morning, Boys," was rich with tone and with meaning too;

it was no common salutation; we apprehended that we were from this time forth to justify our lives, to apply ourselves early unto wisdom, to dedicate our finest selves to the Grammar School (founded A.D. 1665). His eyes, round and protruding, saw a long way, and could deal with the heaps of books hopefully arranged in defence of idleness. "Good morning, Boys," the enigmatic smile, the pause as he surveyed the unit—and another day of earnest endeavour, of improving the mind, of leaving behind the lusts of the flesh had positively begun. At the summit of the vision behind the smile I suppose that there glittered generations of his pupils fulfilling all that he had done for them in higher spheres; for usually in the next place, beaming on us most bewitchingly, though I never fathomed the meaning of that sudden beatific look, he seated himself at the harmonium, flung his gown back, and flourishingly played and began the singing of this hymn in a manner not to be forgotten:

(*At a great pace*):
Around the throne of GOD a band
Of GLORIOUS ANGELS ever stand;
Bright things they see, bright harps they hold,

(*Very, very slow*):
AND ON THEIR HEADS ARE CROWNS OF GOLD.

When hymn and prayers were done, Samuel (we were soon accustomed to his pride in his name) would go over to his desk, and we were "about to hear a Talk." It was indeed a Homily, on the formation of Character, a something which I could not quite isolate—but it was something to be got if a boy wanted to be someone out in the World —another obscure term for me in those days; and, to judge by the principal allusions and even by the absence of allusions, this Character was not attainable by the frivolous and barren paths of cricket and similar interruptions of the

Real. Next we plodded through the character-building of the Old Testament: Joshua, and David, and—Samuel; there was no doubt about it at the moment—cricket was a long way off from the life that threatened us. At break, which was brief, we started up Rounders or Football with a tennis ball (except that one or two larger boys hovered round the kitchen window adoring the maids); these games, it was understood, were approved by Samuel as quick tonics for the mental system. After a few moments we fell in and marched out of the playground in single file back to our seats and parsing and analysis; duly raising our eyes to the diamond panes of the first window we saw Samuel with his hand at the salute, scrutinising his infantry. I wonder if he had at some period read Milton's tractate on Education.

Of an afternoon he would not make so punctual an appearance, and we were less academic; part of the time was often to be spent in filling a quarto page in our book stamped Diary. For me at least this was not the easiest of jobs. Setting forth with quite a trace of desire to show what Life was doing for me, not to mention Samuel, I could not travel on spiritual and scholastic themes much beyond half-way down the page. Reinforcements were urgently needed. It occurred to me that I could mix the useful and the agreeable by summarising, from my attentive reading of parts of *The Evening News* and *The Daily Telegraph*, the cricket adventures of our county team. And I tried to present the information in such select language as might conceivably make the headmaster compliment me on a tendency towards Character. "A gallant knock by Hubble rescued Kent from disaster at Hull." "Dogged resistance by the tail " . . . It would not do. Back came the book with the blue pencil well and truly struck through these notices and the figures appended, and such comments as "Far too much Cricket" in the margin.

To do him justice, Samuel—my first Welshman—was not missing from Dr. Frank's list of subscribers to the village cricket club, and he at least knew when the county team was to play in the neighbourhood and let us off an afternoon's work to go over to the treat. He had arranged for very cheap tickets. I have even seen him with a grin pick up a bat and pretend to get into an attitude of attack on any bowler, but it ended with a pat on the backside of the nearest boy who was usually a scallywag. If the Grammar School team were to have a match, he would encourage the preparations, but he cared nothing for the results, unless once when a youth who was ordinarily looked on as a silly sort of player without a hope stood up to the situation and alone triumphed. He scarcely ever watched the play; and if he walked that way he made it clear that he was going for a walk. There came a day when he was superintending the Annual Athletic Sports. The boys had asked him to include Throwing the Cricket Ball. Shivering in the bleak meadows, the competitors when this event was due paraded before him and applied to him for the ball. He produced—a croquet ball, a pound in weight, three times as heavy as the kind which was wanted; and to all protests he replied that we should find it a very good ball for practical purposes.

This incident finally convinced me that Samuel, a man of such attainments and faculties, could have existed serenely in a cricketless world, and in a sense was doing so; and the fact that I still remember so much about it shows that I was much impressed. Some will say that had I been more fortunate and stayed longer with him, I should have been saved from a heresy and a waste of time. I doubt it; but even as a child I enjoyed Samuel's point of view. One picture of him was at once quite enchanting, and I felt that it expressed something which ought always to go on. It was at the bathing-pool where a splendid oak crowned a steep little sandy bank, and the waters beneath left their transparent gravel-bed for a deeper channel, deep enough for swimming and diving. Under the oak in his white hat sat our master, at leisure, while the boys darted in and out of the stream and showed their skill; there he sat, smiling in complete content, perhaps not quite giving up his right of admonishing, but the very image of a man who needed nothing more exciting from life than this sun, those leafy branches, that willow-fringed stream and those happy boys in his care.

Yet my first impressions had come to stay, and in general no local change was arriving to efface them. The summer's return brought the same deeds and delights as before, and my companions had no philosophic doubts about them. Out of the past, by what way I hardly know, one of them starts up whom I have not had in my mind for years—and there was a time when I should have thought it impossible to forget Tom Race. He lived opposite while I was preparing myself for a greater school; he had a grave, pale, slightly oriental face, and the quietest speech; our talks were of all subjects we could waken, books and studies and history and adventure, and I remember that even he discussed cricket with as sweet a seriousness as any other great subject. A few years later and the battlefield had silenced that voice, and I can see Sergeant Race at his last instant just as I saw him coming from his cottage door, a thinker and a doer both. Such men the land breeds.

At the greater school to which I passed, but to which I suspect I took my village with me, the feeling that cricket was immortal and inevitable was sustained, for we had plenty of it at every possible moment and place. The skilful and the unskilful were all in it; it seemed as a spectacle entirely appropriate to our wide stretches of green under a sky that surely had fewer clouds than skies do now; and although I might have found among the masters some who would have had us spend the summer time in other than cricket fields, I had no inclination to part from a pleasure and an ordeal that had grown up with me. After all, youth has energy and inquiry enough for quite a variety of devotions at the same time. At least I was shy of becoming the slave of cricket, and when there was some prospect of my doing so with the object of excelling, a rustic instinct was there to keep me clear. My heart was still as greatly set on the country itself, on the poetry in which it had been interpreted, on the poems in which I had begun to try for interpretations of my own, as upon any cricket colours; but my behaviour at the nets when the best coaching was offered me should have been a little less incoherent. I could not have pretended by way of excuse that I had been persuaded by the example of Samuel; it was too late for that; but possibly the old gentleman's peculiarities had fashioned me more than I knew.

In any case, did it matter much? The cricket season was rapidly approaching which would be cut short by a war of unimagined rage and reach. I do not think that I ever attained, in boyish simplicity or in later infatuation, the standard of cricket faith of which an indication or two can be traced in that classic, *Wisden's Cricketer's Almanack* for the year 1915. There is something for the satirists in such remarks as were then made on the incidents of August, 1914: "and on August 31, public feeling against the continuance of first-class cricket during the War, having been worked up to rather a high pitch, the committee at a special meeting decided unanimously to cancel the two remaining fixtures. It was in some ways a pity that this drastic step should have been found necessary, but in acting as they did the committee took a wise course. Only two days before the decision was arrived at, Lord Roberts, in a recruiting speech, had made a pointed reference to people who went on playing cricket at such a time."

However, my comment on the early environment and scene of life which have at length led me into those pages, and on the realisation that these causes were not universal and that our game might be like other tribal customs so far as its necessity went, needs not to be extended into the sphere of recruiting speeches. The young, who had on the whole enjoyed their cricket without speculations and debates, went to war, as they perceived that their duty was there. I do not know distinctly what feelings of nostalgia prevail this time in the breasts of those admirable successors now holding the line, but as for the last generation, a short poem written at the time by one of them instantly pierced me through with its truth, and that truth seemed to be most pointed in one Wordsworthian line:

> I see them in foul dug-outs, gnawed by rats,
>   And in the ruined trenches, lashed with rain,
> Dreaming of things they did with balls and bats ...

When I first read the line, it seemed to me to throw all the argument for or against the English game to the winds, and it still tells me an intense truth about the old front line. The writer of the poem, *Dreamers*, will be met again as I proceed.

III

Then and Now

CRICKETERS who are reading these pages might like to have me look back and try to compare the character of the game as it went in Edwardian years and villages with its recent condition. I cannot pretend to make this comparison well, but one general difference has struck me, though it is not copyright: the game right on the green or in the alley has become more professional. That is, the village player has been educating himself more and more in the science of it. Great performers arrange courses of instruction in the winter months which the boy with the motor-cycle, and rather more money than he would have had in 1900 or 1910, can easily profit by. The big matches are more extensively discussed in print, especially by famous cricketers turned authors, who admit us almost to the holy of holies in their outlook on the strategy of the game and on the incidents of particular techniques. And then on the air Mr. Howard Marshall (his name may stand for all, the master name) makes every ball bowled, every shifting of a fieldsman so fertile with meaning that any wireless set make may a subtle cricket student of anybody.

So when you see our village side in action nowadays— forgive me if in my fancy I do not always treat the War as quite so permanent—you can easily ask, and I heard one of the old first eleven turned spectator ask with a will, "Why pay to see first-class cricket?" The illusion is, at least it can be clever; you might be looking at a county side in preparation. The very caps are worn as if the wearers announced their allegiance to the world's chosen best; the bats swing on the line of beauty, the bowler hints and prompts his fieldsmen a yard this way and that, the young expert snatches the run at the end of the over to keep a doubtful

comrade away from the bowling, in accordance with the
theories obtaining "up aloft." Now all this may have fixed
a gulf between our village cricket now, with its hitters of
scintillating centuries, and the sporadic games which I have
tried to picture, dear to children and some children of larger
growth, perhaps the relics of really ancient pastimes of
hedger and ditcher. This worthy, however, may yet upset
the clever work of the progressives, for the one thing in
cricket that cannot be taught, in the long run, is bowling.
"Nature's above Art in that respect." We have our lissom
willow-wielders, and four after four curving through the
covers or hooked round from the off stick decorates the play
and sends up the score; but people, and not only old people,
look down their noses when some one starts a talk on the
bowlers. Those we have do not lack grace or method, but
by contrast with those of the old school they have no devil
in them, no shrewd rage. The primitive is the essence of
bowling—I should put Caliban on at both ends if I could.
The cry is all for a "hostile bowler." But in these times
I am half afraid that Caliban would have been seduced from
his twisters and shooters and extra fast ones, and would be
ambitiously cultivating his batsmanship with the help of
Don Bradman's text and pictures. His observation:

> "I'll be wise hereafter
> And seek for Grace"

must relate to a former desire of improvement.

I have been speaking of some things which a small tally
of years has made as remote as the island which Caliban
once ruled ; the expected happens but does not grow easier
to accept; I have felt with grief and amazement how the
actors on that little stage of cricket turf which drew our
plaudits "the other day" have been hastening out of the
world. The very graves of some of them have a Gray's
Elegy look already. That dry-tongued, punctilious, restless,
happy Hon. Sec., who had not served with a regiment in
India without taking a certain impression never to be

effaced, has long shared a tomb with his two sisters—maiden ladies, who had grown old without repining. Their world exacted seventy years of spinsterhood from so many a laughing girl. He had his cricket, they their church duties, all three a friendly outlook on destiny and human nature. Since the Hon. Sec.'s scratchy kindly salutation is heard no more, and the moss gathers and painted snail climbs on his glimmering cross, it is not strange that most of the teams he collected are gone also. But I have not yet accustomed my inner self to the change. The slashing batsman and tearaway fast bowler ought surely not to have been, in so brief a time, converted into a gentle invalid and then a name; and his wife, whose rose-petal beauty used to enhance for me even the sweetness of the fancy-cakes she brought round among the children under the young sycamore, how has she been captured by age and death? But there is no unwinding this queer process, which fascinates philosophers and scientist and poets, and makes every one of us one day see, like a new face in our mirror, that our closest sentry-go on our affairs and campaigns missed the arch-Antic, or Illusion, or Dimension. I grant that Time as he is traditionally figured bears some likeness to our village cricket groundsman, at least the old one who knew not the motor mower:

> "Great enimy to . . . all the rest
> That in the *Gardin* of *Adonis* springs
> Is wicked *Time*, who with his scyth adrest
> Does mow the flowring herbes and goodly things,
> And all their glory to the ground downe flings."

Annually the Hon. Sec., like myriads of his kind throughout the British Empire, used to edit a neat little cardboard folder, recording the ranks and dignities of the C.C., the season's results, and the averages of the players—both teams. Like more magnificent and comprehensive periodical works, this one has become very hard to get, and under some circumstances this is as well. One of the old style of our cricketers who does not take much notice of his advancing age can sometimes be found of an evening, in fair weather, in the seat of honour in the private bar of The Flower Pot, where he holds a harmless court, and judges this world and wishes it would learn. With an artist's instinct (he himself might use the words about others) he has gradually reconsidered his cricket life—has selected, has taken the better part of fortune; and now in his conception and his narration it is approaching what it should have been. I say, it is as well that none of the boys is now likely to pick up a copy of one of the old Hon. Sec.'s annual registers. What are dull statistics worth in comparison with the idea in its celestial hues? Those figures which our reminiscent friend occasionally drops in, to assist our attention and to honour the use of history, are never pressed with rigidity: "Let's see, I took my bat out for something round fifty, wasn't it, Charlie? forty it may have been—any road it was near enough fifty." Alas for me, my recollection goes back to the seasons over which he has drawn the flowery gauzes of hope clearly enough to suspect long ago that good old Zachary had not hit up quite enough runs for greatness. The Hon. Secretary was horribly accurate, and in his annual the relevant line used to run somewhat like this:

Name	No. of Innings	Times Not Out	Aggregate	Best Score	Average
Z. Whibble	17	4	129	28[1]	9.9

The years have instructed me to some extent in the art of keeping silence where truth is a declaration of war, so I listen to the visions of Zachary as calmly as Charlie does; and as he used to turn out regularly under Z.'s captaincy, but has no particular notion how he fared in any one match, he sometimes gets a reward. He is reminded (the cup is put down for a moment) that he too was in Arcadia that day, and although it must be said that he did not for his part accumulate the notches, yet his steady play was indispensable to Zachary's doing so. Moreover, when it came to

[1] Signifies Not Out.

their turn as bowlers . . . I am glad that one or two of the boys cannot work on these heartening sagas in the manner of Mr. Blotton defying Samuel Pickwick. For they are a little inclined to cricket mathematics. They go wrong that way too, I fancy. Zachary's aggregate for an entire season would not perhaps equal the best single score of some of them ; and perhaps none of them could have stayed to make 15 runs as he did one afternoon, several afternoons, on some appalling downhill wicket with a large wrathful swerve-bowler using the wind and the black sky and waving trees behind him, to the immediate rude destruction of all save Zachary.

The "mellowing glass" of memory may be false to detail and yet delightful; but the vanishing of all circumstances from a man's mind is a sad matter. The ancient man who had been a young visitor to the Great Exhibition, 1851, when I sat next to him evening upon evening in 1931, remembered only that he remembered it. Even that I suspect depended on someone telling him his duty. I am sorry to surmise that if my life is prolonged in the same way, I shall be in very much the same unentertaining condition. Youth will await my picturesque impression of K. S. Ranjitsinjhi and his leg-glide, or perhaps of the Fourth of August, 1914, and the end of an era, and I shall promptly mumble with grim pride, "Yes, I saw the Prince bat—he was an Indian gentleman, you know," "Yes, that was the day one of the Wars broke out—I was told about it." Indeed, even now, I can hardly offer anything like a sunlight moment when I may be tempted to mention that I saw R. H. Spooner at the Oval. He made 224 runs, Lancashire altogether 360—that much survives; it was an innings of grace and strength—you all know that; he stood nobly tall, easy, untired in manner, all through—you would expect that. Studious also—every ball. It was the sunshine of cricket at his end of the pitch, that I feel; for the other end, the batsmen who one after another supported him (a little), are all in shadow now.

If any benefactor offers a prize for a clear memory, there is a candidate in our parish. When I was last able to take my seat at The Flower Pot—for even now there are some in those cottages who do not count me as altogether an exile —a gentleman came in whom I recognised by degrees as one of the occasional bass singers in the long-lost heroic era of our village choir and concert. I did not quite like it at first when he discovered us, as a family circle, talking of cricket in the day of battle, but he was not frowning over that ; it was the small range of our recollections that troubled him. So he took up the subject, and detailed several mighty performances (his own not overlooked) on the part of our cricket teams in the past. They were so mighty, and his appearance so youthful, that I was perplexed at not having such records engraved on the tablet of my own memory. Someone asked him pensively when these local cricket masterpieces happened. "In the Nineties," he answered simply, as though that was surely a date we all shared and had in the front of our minds, a mere matter of the calendar.

But what can I say for my own memory? It seemed to undertake a burden for life during the War of 1914-1918— a case which must be far from unique. When I would rescue some exact instance of the cricket which was formerly so like earthly paradise to me, and of which perhaps I was an official scorer at twopence a match, the resistance is strong. There is no cure except perhaps future time. Yet I have a general remembrance of the village game, and even if some later influences have imbrowned the colouring I cannot but take my picture as something that I perceived, an aspect of the actual.

A thunderstorm is stooping over the old cricket ground in my memory. It is not a date that I can identify, and I do not know who the awaited opponents of our team are— an Estate, a Brewery, the Constabulary, some sort of Rovers, more likely just another village side. It is the forenoon, and that inky cloud is working round the hill, as black almost as the spinney of firs on the boundary, imported trees which I always suspect of being aloof in their hearts from the scene and its animations. I feel oily splashing drops and doubt if we shall have the promised encounter in the afternoon. The summer seems to have fallen into low spirits, and there is nobody about except the rooks and pigeons—we have heard all they have to say—and a crying woodpecker down under the oak at the river. The storm drifts, the cloud-edges are effaced; but the rain patters steadily on the metal roof of the mowing shed, the gutters gurgle, all the trees are grey with the shower. Past the far side of the field a figure with a sack for hood drives his cycle apace, never turning his eyes this way for a moment; and no one from the vicarage steps out to see if there is any prospect of play.

Yet the hours pass, and after all the rain has wearied, and stopped. The smoky-looking day may remain thus, neither better nor worse, and the turf is good. A bicycle is being pushed through the meadow gate by a cricketer in flannels under his mackintosh, and one by one they all assemble. An unlocking of padlocks and shifting of benches in the pavilion, a thump of bats and stumps being hauled out of the dark corners. The creases are marked, and the offer of a bowling screen rejected. Our boys put catapults back in their jackets and affect to know personally the visitors now arriving, pointing out one or two with awe —that one who hits sixes, and that one with the spectacles who never scores less than seventy. There are not many cricket caps on show, and some of the players are observed to feel safest with braces and ties on.

Sawdust wanted! The fielding side have spread themselves about the soaked ground, and all is otherwise ready —even the two batsmen have gone out to their creases, casting rather unhappy looks on their companions in the pavilion, who sit down in a row and brood. It is odd, this serious game; perhaps it is the greyness of the day that causes it to take this mood. Sawdust ! A bucket is being carried forth by the groundsman, whose squat shoulders and beard look like the picture of Hudibras; he tips out his two little mounds of sawdust, and marches off to his shed, as who should say, "That is the end of the match for me. That *is* the match." The one-armed bowler measures his run, dips the ball into the sawdust, and with three or four sharp steps whizzes it at the opposed batsman; it passes with a wet smack into the gloves of the man behind the stumps. All the fieldsmen attend gravely. This bowler has pace. But no smile.

But the ball won't turn and after a time the batsman lose their reverence and risk sending it over the head of the little man at point; the score is hoisted, and the bowlers are changed. It is mainly that schoolboy who is the cause of this. His score in the book is inspected, it adds up to 18 already. He looks too delicate to perform among these rugged elders, but he is calm enough. At last a large hand and circling arm send him a ball which sails up very much like the one before which he carted over peering faces into the long wet grass; it falls shorter, hits him on the boot. He knows his offence, and the umpire does not let him off; but his innings has gone far enough. There are several batsmen to follow him, and already the total is one which in these games of strong trundlers may serve—50 up. The boy who has seen to this matter and accepted the punishment for his single error so immediately goes walking away there, with his hands stuck into his green jacket, as if on Robinson Crusoe's island, to the far parts of the field. He seems to have this cricket business in his pocket. When he was questioned just now as he put his pads away "what the bowling was like," he answered slowly and peacefully, "The fellow from the lower end turns them a little from the off."

The circuit of the field which falls away to the stream is wide enough for him to be still strolling and watching the blue moths among the sorrel when the downfall of the last of his team mates arrives. It was not so easy out there as he found it. These men with the ball have a terrible natural skill. Perhaps it is not mere talk, that they can drop it on a threepenny bit placed between the wickets. They can probably hit a rat with a turnip in the light of their lantern before he knows that he is in the way.

But here is the second part of the game, and the relaxation of the interval dies into another period of silent close watching. Only about 75 runs are necessary, but those who are to try for them do not look exactly merry at the prospect. The church clock tolls out again, five o'clock; it always comes to the hour slower, speaks it in a lower tone than that brisk silver-voiced one at the grange. In the pavilion a faint notion goes that "if we can't get the runs we may make a draw of it"; but half-past six under the circumstances is a good way off. Once again in the sulky light against the gloomy trees the bowlers appear the dangerous persons of the drama as they strike their heels in, start their run and slam the ball at their opponents; the stiff farmer and the patient gardener, though their chins express refusal to be less than British, do not quite treat their bats as natural extensions of themselves. As their admirers the boys look at their narrow escapes, there are inevitable gaspings. Meanwhile someone looks away from the torture for a moment and directs attention to two youths in the next field: youths who ought to have been playing here, and who are credited with ability equal to any bowler's attack in the world; and these are on their way unconcernedly to bream swims with rods and baskets and landing nets. A case of defection, too sad to be dwelt upon, but it all goes with this slow grey day.

The home team is in trouble. The curate from whom (on the old principle "omne ignotum pro magnifico") at least a few wristy educated shots were expected on his first appearance here, has just had his bails flicked off, very hard luck; and the side is half out. The score-board is not our study now. Moreover, Mr. Warrener won't get his innings; he has received a message from his master, General Goble, who surely could not have sent for him at this (familiar) crisis except on account of some truly grave emergency. A boy, however, is walking out to the captain of the fielding side, to supplicate for leave to bat instead of the confidential Warrener. The captain grins, pulls the boy's ear and says yes. The boy comes back with an attempt to be neutral about it, "It's all in the day's work," but he feels alarmed, and things all round are grey.

Bert Pilgrim, who has a rich curly head of bronze hair, goes and confronts the bowlers. He takes a bat which is so chewed up—the only spare one too—that only he (it suits him) uses it in a match. He does not use it long, but he operates it much as when he tries his strength at the Flower Show with the maul which drives a block up a tall post, to ring a bell and return the penny if bumped hard enough. He gets one boundary off the dodging umpire's backside and a six in the homely equipage of the old woman selling popcorn, liquorice straps and still lemonade. The score is not improved enough in spite of all this, and Bert comes back again rather grumpy because a very old gentleman, as he sees age, has wrought his downfall with the very kind of bowling he prays for to his heathen gods. The ancient, belted in several faded colours round a massive central contour, first took leave to bowl a few gentle ones up and down aside from the wicket, while the batsman affected indifference. Such was the fashion of those unhaggling days, though it was going. Then to the game again. The ball was coming up so mildly, but it evaded Bert's punitive swing, he glared round, the bails fell, he said something. And another one. The end is in sight; some restless man begins putting away the tackle lying about—and the boy who bats in place of Mr. Warrender finds himself going in. "Just you stay there." But "over" was called. In his neat shoes polished like his locks for the match, the boy stands prepared to run any number of runs. 'Poggy' at the far end puts his bat to the ball—the boy is called: "no, yes, go back, come on"—and with a little pause of compassion and shame the bowler, ball in hand, breaks the wicket at the boy's end. He pats him on the shoulder, which is Fame enough. The match is finished, stumps are pulled up; players withdraw from the place, leaving two sawdust patches and some tracks of trampled mud for the alighting rook to investigate. And at last the western sky glows into a little colour, like the streaks on the honeysuckle by the glistening hedge which the players and their friends pass on their way to strong tea and plum cake in their homes. We shall not be very well pleased to find the match reported in next week's *Messenger*.

So runs this once-upon-a-time in my memory, which as I admitted I do not acquit of growing old along with me; yet perhaps it has not given an altogether wrong evidence on this subject. The cricket was all rather a grave affair. I suppose it was the weather mostly that made it so, and any one from abroad who knows the prevailing summer gloom surrounding a landing at Dover may concur. But the game gave me some sense of being rather a continuation of rural labours than a sport and pastime. It was carried through as earnestly as, say, measuring the hops in a bin, or bringing a team of horses over the bridge with that queer thing a car steering along from the other direction; where there was skill, it was applied with the same attentiveness as the skill of grafting a tree. Perhaps it was the weather, I say to myself again, and there must have come another day, and come many a time, when the laughing sky was reflected in the light-hearted frolics and gaieties of my old country cricketers. Not even thus can I find a way from their habit of cricket, a hard game. They were too firmly fixed within necessities of toil and shrewdness, duty and plainness, to be easily renewed in a short interlude as children of the sun. Their cricket was of another mood from that which would be played on the same ground a few days later by those whose tradition was polished entertainment, the social round, the glorious indolence of a "modest competence" or a small fortune.

Among the Moderns

A TALLISH, striding youth who gave the impression of being short of small talk was among the visiting players on our ground, in the matches of the First Eleven. It is not surprising that he was reserved in manner, for he had a secret that would not have been readily detected or understood, I imagine, by his companions; his private hours were devoted largely to writing poetry. This peculiarity has led to his becoming famous, but it is in prose that he has given a view of the cricket we saw, if the match in his *Memoirs* is rightly considered to be partly pictured from one of ours. S. Sassoon was, and still is, a cricketer of ability, and a student of the game. He played in the company of some whose names were more resplendent to us—certainly more familiar—than those of the heroes of war, and politics, and the world's affairs in general. I think I remember of a photograph of him in proximity to the immortal Colin Blythe and Hardinge.

In idle speculation I wish that this poet could have led into the field a team consisting of other English poets versed in the game. There would be his favourite Cowper—I owe to S.S. my proper regard for *The Needless Alarm*—W. Cowper, once the pride of Westminster cricket. Lord Byron, if he was not busy otherwise, taking boxing lessons or swimming the Hellespont, should be on the bowling strength. Perhaps it would be winked at if the Hon. L. H. Tennyson represented his tuneful grandfather, and Christopher Wordsworth did the same for his uncle (but Christopher too was a poet if we do not exclude religious verse as a qualification); and then Robert Bridges should appear in person, and in exquisite flannels—one of our chief hopes with the bat. S.S.

would know if the allusions of his dear George Meredith to cricket arose from direct achievement, and got him a place other than at the edge of the field. Of parson George Crabbe there is no doubt; wherever he and his boys on a free day could find a bit of smooth grass it is recorded that they pitched their stumps. Some may not remember that Conan Doyle was a poet and a cricketer as well as the inventor of Sherlock Holmes and Dr. Watson; but *Songs of Action* and a gift as a bowler, exhibited formerly on our ground and many others, bring him in. The umpiring of Francis Thompson, the score-keeping of Gerard Manley Hopkins, would have been of a distinctive kind; and among the close supporters and the parasols I see Miss Mitford, charmed more than she meant to be with the conversation of Leigh Hunt. He has come partly because he thinks it a "manly" sport and means to philosophise, but really to watch John Keats, who is a neat long-stop. But I must not indulge my fond day-dream any longer, with these "souls of poets dead and gone" haunting the green and making unromantic remarks on the fernweed and dock invading the sacred arena. There are living lyrists who would be with them. I select them all, I am sure that S.S. would be their skipper, and will have just the private word for every one of them.

He has now captained for several years a country cricket team which stands for the best that the game can yield. In its flourishing one may discern a parallel to his poetry, that part of it at least which utters his sense of things natural and rural and their lasting pre-eminence. There is no misty sentiment in this his standing upon the ancient ways, but clear judgment only; no philosophic doubt whether change is bad, but a resolution that some changes ought not to be done in a hurry. Vicissitude can be counted on to unsettle many long-accepted and valued institutions, but S.S. is not pressing forward to assist this deity who needs no man's help. So at any rate I read his unspoken thoughts. At a period when Estate is in some disfavour we may well understand why he has chosen it, much in its old form; and while the world echoes with systems, new societies, governances and proposals for them he continues his practical creed of the country house with as much as is workable of its locally useful influence. He can let his meadows, plant his woodland, employ husbandry, preside on occasions, be the friend of the village, study his literary and artistic concerns, and entertain and refresh the minds of others who share those interests. Included in his little principality, as it always used to be in such places, is the cricket ground—and the proper name of the team is still the Estate C.C. Let toast-masters remember this.

I can fancy that someone may demur at this, or at my notion or expression of it, and if so I will make him a present of a quotation from Francis Bacon, *Of Innovations*. The essayist observes that customary things "are as it were confederate within themselves: whereas New Things peece not so well," and after some more considerations like that he says, "All this is true, if Time stood still; which contrariwise moveth so round, that a Froward Retention of Custome is as turbulent a Thing, as an *Innovation*: And they that Reverence too much Old Times, are but a Scorne to the New." But I cannot detect a "froward retention" in S.S. The polite but severe use of the theory "Clay from clay differs in dignity" which I have known even on cricket grounds is nothing of his. Easy leadership, good done "by stealth" is his contribution, and if these courses are out of date Nature has been doting. From the fireside talks of "committees" in small villages I ever remember the wish that someone would come and live there who had this leadership—"The chaps are all wanting to do something, but it's a shame there's nobody to give them a lead."

All my disquisitions on this theme and any defensiveness that they suggest would be unnecessary if we could instantly join S.S.'s team for an afternoon there in the Wylye valley. "A sylvan scene," his ground alone ought to soothe and subdue even detraction. It has been menaced by plans of

strategic road making and the like, but prayers and inter-
views and correspondence have so far saved it. For a few
people to play a game? For the happy leisure of a village—
men, women, even babies who just come or are carried
hither because a cricket match in the right weather with
such grass and flowers and trees is able to drive care away.
No sweeter hours are given. The players are various in age,
in trade and calling, in ability; but a common courtesy
unites them, and they understand cricket apart from their
individual performances. If I gave them another quotation
from Bacon they would ratify it: "They be two things,
Unity and *Uniformity*." They fight out its battles, as they
are fighting out this war, not for lust of conquest nor pride
of place but for the light of an idea. Perhaps T., and G.,
if they heard me talking like this, would feel faintly alarmed,
but T. would help me out by saying, as he has done, "Cricket's
a Game." And Mrs. Battle would please both him and G.
by taking up the plain word and transferring her interest
a moment from the card-table to these matches in Wiltshire:
"They are a sort of dream-fighting; much ado; great
battling, and little bloodshed; mighty means for dispro-
portioned ends; quite as diverting, and a great deal more
innoxious, than many of those more serious *games* of life,
which men play, without esteeming them to be such."

When the woeful hunting of War is let loose, cricket
cannot escape the prevailing fate of all pleasant things, and
its charm is even less recoverable at such times than that
of things less passionately adored. "The Greater Game"
appals this one, not merely driving it from its field but
making it hard to read of or talk about. I have lately, in the
fourth year of the Greater War, glanced through some of
Wisden's scores of important matches, but could not bring
myself to do this until now, and even now the figures and
the narrative mocked me. They had a dead look. This was
not a new experience. In the trenches in May, 1916, I
remembered that the cricket season should have just begun,
but the thought died in me almost as soon as it was born.

The essence of cricket is subtle, and I did not feel under that burden of destruction and vast decision that its complex sources would ever be well re-created. A few days later a sergeant of my platoon, who already made me more than usually diffident over my hopes of being of any use, mentioned cricket and, leaning against the sandbags, six feet of him, gazed cheerfully, carelessly into space. I asked him, as he intended I should, what exactly he used to do as a cricketer; and he got started on that. His highest score, it came out, was 173. But as usual he rather prided himself on being a bowler, though I got no details of corresponding successes in that branch. Naturally he carried himself with a certain pride. But I fear he did not survive the next battle. After this I seldom heard any cricketana, though so many had had the game by heart, throughout the war. In the home camp towards the end a few of us once got out the bat and ball. But what did it signify? Even when the guns had ceased fire, I could not come back to cricket for a season or two; and I think cricket itself did not come back all at once. It had been dismayed; it did not guess in the golden days at things like world wars, or that the score-books should be splashed with the blood of the quiet men its votaries.

Will the case be the same, or worse, when this new war is done? Besides, we were made increasingly restless and undecided before it began with clamours about the need for reforming cricket. Certainly there were odd extremes in the course of the big matches. The English side, meeting the world's best bowler on a wicket that did nothing wrong, and the world's most agile fieldsmen to help him, made over nine hundred runs and were still in a position to add a hundred or two when Mr. Hammond declared the innings closed. Now I cannot explain why, but cricketers feel that a score of a thousand runs is the ruin of the match, as a primrose a foot in diameter would spoil primroses. On the other hand, in South Africa, the English batsmen were set about seven hundred runs to make for victory in the fourth innings. A fantasy—except that in the dressing-room they said, Why not? They almost achieved the fantasy, but before they could quite conjure it into reality, the tenth day of the match was over—and cricketers feel that for matches to last ten days is the ruin of the game. Even epics must not be timeless Tests. But what is to come of the distaste and suspicions of so many judges? In the progress of cricket science there can be no artificial pause consonant with the health of the game in its major form.

The answer or part of it is with the Estate C.C. for or against whom you should play one day—and by this I do not imply that they are naïve and short of skill. Far from it. D., that devoted shepherd, comes from the hurdled hillside to the opening of the innings with the watchfulness and power of a master; P. bowls and bats as resourcefully as he has found necessary in a successful local career; and I could go on noting the side's resources. How good young W. G. was getting, before he put on uniform! But as a whole such a side is free from the solemn rule of "digging in" which big cricket prescribes, and it performs without sense of restraint inside the time of a long afternoon. For these, it is still a game; and it is neither too ill played to be worth the watching nor too double-sure to be other than a series of impeccable displays. The sun and shade ripple round its players, dogs start out across the pitch with amiable unheeded messages, cuckoos fly after their mates past the bowling screen (I fear S.S. insists on mounting that, but "it is a very little one") and if it is one of the high days hallowed by a lunch in the House no one fasts from fear that anything he eats might lead to his being out for less than 200.

"L'accordéon s'est tu dans le pays des mines."

So the poet of North-east France tells us in this war, and his words linger. The music of the matches played in sight of S.S.'s lofty windows is condemned to a main silence also, and I grieve for both these victims of the time; yet in a few years perhaps I shall be fortunate enough to pass from one to the other, from the little but vociferous estaminets of Lens and Auchel to the seat on the boundary at H——y, resting my spirits in the enjoyment of seeing people naturally enjoying their own traditions. The last time that I saw S.S.'s team in action, it was perhaps the best on which the series should close for a time. The other side was one of a rather different composition—I speak as one who has been associated with it throughout its happy life; and this difference may be the secret of the unbroken serenity of the relationship between the two teams. They are complementary. I will call this other side the Paladins; there are many such in our Universities, and I hope I do not infringe a copyright in a title. *These* Paladins spring in principle from the brain of an eminent Ciceronian at Oxford, a classical tutor noted for his ability to score Firsts in final examinations, any examinations, through the medium of all and sundry committed to his charge. One day, laying aside his set books, R. gazed through his spectacles into the future, and saw ranged before him many cricket grounds, and many cricketers, and himself leading a part of those on many a sunny Saturday to the combat. He accepted the vision, and the captaincy, and action followed. We have always thought of him since in something like the terms of a conspicuous declaration by Virgil:

> I am the man who once professed the Muse,
> And taught youth's vacant wilderness to yield;
> But now I cultivate my Cricket Blues,
> And march my blazer'd warriors on the field.

But the Paladins are not all cricketers of the star class, nor all so young as they would like to be. The recruiting of the team is various, and among its mysteries is the fact that its illustrious players when they come in do not necessarily take the honours. But then, for a good part of the season the matches are played in bucolic conditions announcing the invincibility of agricultural freedom; though cow and donkey after a little parley amble off reluctantly to let the silly old stuff begin. I have sometimes, on such cricket grounds, harboured faint doubts as to the entirety of the truth of Fitzgerald's stanza:

> The Ball no Question makes of Ayes and Noes,
> But Right or Left as strikes the Player goes;
> And He that toss'd Thee down into the Field,
> *He* knows about it all—HE knows—HE knows!

For even players who have lately produced a faultless innings against a champion county may strike right or left on the cow-pasture at Dankbury-by-the-Mere, and afterwards note that the ball had its own contrary views where to go, if go it did. And as for someone with ball in hand unchangingly able to predict where it would fly on leaving it and pitching among the hummocks at Dankbury I am equally uncertain.

Still, I was very much struck by the foreknowledge of one old man, possibly the same that Fitzgerald had word of, who sat in his usual corner stolidly watching one of the Paladins' most upland matches. At one time I wondered if this match would ever take place, for after we with all our deplorable baggage had discovered the stile-path to the ground an immense and cold-hearted gander flanked by several other creatures barred the way. However, he slowly retreated, his blue eye still asserting his disapproval, and we entered the chilly and miry field. The home team came scrambling at the last minute over gate and hedge, and presently Paladins in fine raiment went in to bat. Some of them did not get enough of it to tire of it, and when the village bowlers had done with them the total was about 43. Penury indeed. It was at that point that I thought it safe to address words to the stolid old man, and I said with becoming shame (and yet indicating the greatness of Dankbury cricket) that it was a miserable score. He did not agree.

He replied, "'Tis a winning score, Mister, on this here pitch there's no team gets up to that." Dankbury now batted. Our glorious fast bowler, whose eye as he begins his rush at the batsman is even more hostile than that of the aforesaid gander, scored the first five or six runs for Dankbury when his ball struck some quartz or iron deposit in the middle of the pitch, soared over the small wicket-keeper's head and the grasp of two or three acrobats behind him, and then bounded eerily hither and thither into a small slough. Orders were then given by R. that T. should reduce his speed by half, but even so the devil was in it, and T. was soon displaced for a less expensive slinger. To be brief, that afternoon the ball did as *it* chose, the home batsmen came and went in a procession—sadder even than the Paladins, and the mossy old man's prediction was comfortably right when every one left the ground for a warmer corner. HE knows; but he is not always available. Well, thinking it over, I have a feeling that he may be.

"Charles," I said to the only international cricketer whom I have the daring to call by his Christian name, "one day, won't you come and play for the Paladins?" Scenting the rich humours of village cricket, the ripe Dickensian adventure and the bacchanalia, he very kindly said that he would; and as always he kept his promise. I do not think that a better bowler of his type lives, except always that other schoolmaster W. J. O'Reilly. In the course of the talk from which I quoted, I had asked him another question, maybe rather a grim one to ask; had he ever felt in the county matches that his bowling had been really and truly collared? He thought it over with the aid of his pipe, and said that he did not remember such an extremity, apart from a period or two when the batsmen did things to his best ones. So to the match in which this grand bowler joined the Paladins. It was Sunday, it was Sussex, and (on the rector's intimation) stumps were to be drawn before the church bells began for evensong. The ground was outstretched and narrow, and the pitch was not sited far from the highroad crossing the green at one end. The pitch was not unkempt but it was visibly a pitch of character. Charles opened the attack for the Paladins at the highroad end, and I felt penitently that any of the local boys who had set eyes on his armorial blazer and seen cricketer written all over him before the game started might be almost too overawed to proceed.

So Charles began on a dance-step of danger, with his usual life and fire, and the ball whipped across in a fierce hurry; but the batsmen did not seem unduly surprised. They knew the geography or the demonology just there. Balls did whip across. The first wicket fell after a quiet, pleasant partnership, the new batsman was short and sturdy of build and at first I half suspected him of being Maurice Leyland in disguise—their reply to our stratagem of bringing Charles. He took guard, stepped back and examined the field, surveyed the country behind the bowler, and stood ready for the ball. A moment or two later he clouted Charles's well-concealed fast one into the air, and it struck the highroad like a mortar bomb. This did not seem to surprise the hitter either; and he went on doing it or things very similar. "Who is that fellow?" he turned and asked me meditatively while the ball was being retrieved from a stable yard, as though he had detected a touch of originality in the bowling which deserved some credit. Perhaps I was actually being unsportsmanlike in answering, "I'll tell you afterwards." Poor Charles could not solve the problem of getting this smiter caught in the deep field with so short a boundary, and meanwhile the score was going up quite uncomfortably for so short an afternoon's cricket. R. very tactfully desired Charles to try if the other end would suit him better; the trial was made, but the village knew something that way too. I ought to hush up the story, or say it like the boy in the *Winter's Tale*—"yond crickets shall not hear it,"—but it is all a joyous memory now. The sons of the green all made hay. The Paladins were sent in to get an impossible number of runs before the coming of the parson's hour, and had to stick their bats dolefully in the way of some terrific fast ones unconcealed by art, while Charles waited with his pads on for the innings which never came.

And all that is only a thing that we enjoyed the other day. "Are the white hours for ever fled?" and is all our company dispersed for ever? Even without a war they were the kind of young men, the Paladins, who are impelled to take responsibility and try fortune in distant parts of the world. Such was R——n, tall and free of limb, whose truly ingenious bowling was adapted to village grounds, and batting too—for when he took his bat forth he aimed at neighbouring railway embankments and the like. He had a beautiful lazy way of entering the game, whether it was a simple one or more exacting. He would be holding a stem of grass in his teeth as he grabbed the ball, tied a bootlace tighter and waved a fieldsman where he needed him. He seldom discussed the details of the cricket, grinning at it all and at this world's more extensive variations. By divine right the horizon was his. Not unlike him was another of our bowlers whom we could not hope to have with us so often, since he was inevitably claimed by our superiors: but D. was a little different from R. in his indolent seeming. He also, tall and easy, bowled with an air of just playing with a ball, of liking it, as a child with a doll; but he set a value on spare moments, and in big games when he was fielding without much immediate work on the boundary you saw him making the obvious use of a deserted deck chair, or talking to the boys and giving them the names of the players and asking them theirs. He might have been merely dealing with our old friends at Chainstreet Excelsior when he was keeping the Australians themselves uncommonly quiet, in the days of their most intimidating achievement. What a very slow ball it looked to us that he served up to Mr. Bradman, who flashed his bat for a predestined six over the square leg boundary; but the ball did not tower, indeed it sneaked through to the batsman's pads, and some will always bear witness that the umpire's finger went up just before the contact! "What was the secret?" we asked D. of course, whose name had thus become historic (in this branch of history). "Straight ball," he replied. For him too the skyline held a fascination as he sat down, a cricketer of class who saw in this universe a long way beyond the fall of wickets.

"Pray you, mark; that is a very noble youth." It has sometimes been my feeling as I watched some of these Paladins in their glowing, singing springtime of life, clad in the agreeable uniform of our game, walking and talking in free companionship, that they are characters who have come to life out of some Elizabethan drama speaking of a code of honour. Names like Amintor and Philaster seem properly to belong or to have belonged to them, and to the courtliness of their parts in this scene of cricket. They could wear swords and draw them in a cause that cried for such a service, but I like them with their bats best, and these were wont to flash brightly enough in our bloodless arguments. As I catch the gleam of these high-spirited boys and their dexterities in the lists and jousts of past summers, I feel that they have not changed, and needed not, now that they are serving in the wars with the modern equivalents of the sword. Too frank to disguise "the image and horror of it" or to affect a superiority to fears and disillusionings, they will carry with them that inward light which so pleased and charmed me when we were together on our former occasions. Even amidst the worst confusion they will carry the day with their brilliance—a look, a smile, a gesture, a comment of theirs will lead their company beyond the apparent battle. For a philosophy of life, I say let us listen to Youth.

Yet not all are there now; once again even the daisied path of cricket leads into the place of untimely graves. While still this war was very young, while it was scarcely disclosed, and those who were in training for it had a little leisure, the Paladins played a match or two, and at one of these a young master of batsmanship already established in big cricket was one of the opponents. He came in to open the innings as usual, but not as usual—it seemed that he had not been able to collect his cricket boots, and he grinned at the wicket-keeper in apology for his gym shoes. Another Yorkshireman, our pace bowler T., prepared to bowl against him or against anybody.

The second ball which T. catapulted down, swung out, the batsman flicked at it, and tipped it into a pair of philosophical hands behind. He grinned again with a sense of the justice of this result as he turned back to the pavilion. This, I believe, was the last ball ever played by this sterling cricketer, and at the time my relief at seeing him go for 1 instead of 100 was curiously mixed with a sadness. The war is older now, and already the news of this boy's death (one of the early list) might belong to some other war.

When our fast bowlers have not been on their day, we have had the advantage of a very slow one indeed, who is no other than R. himself. It is always a period of doubt among his followers, even of mutinous or involved whisperings, when it becomes evident that R. is thinking of putting himself on to bowl. The thought of what might happen to the score in one or two of his overs, if the hitters ranged against us should get hold of them, is severe. Yet his bowling, which scarcely looks likely in mechanics to arrive at the other wicket, at least not in a one-day match, has very often upset all calculations. He applies to the problem the same nicely of judgment as he brings to that of converting mankind into classical scholars. Batsmen, watching that languid run up, that drawl (so to speak) of R.'s left arm, that gradual ascent and descent of the ball, think that their guardian angels have been really affable for once; but the tremendous and vain lashings that follow must often supply them with a proof of the existence of devils. Excitement is their quick downfall; and R. has been known to clear out nine batsmen for hardly any more than nine runs, especially in the most undiluted country game. One of these lingers greatly in my sense; it wandered along through an afternoon of warm delicate rain, with feathery woodlands fencing us in from the world of worry, and all the afternoon from the light green coverts the nightingales were singing.

The thought of R.'s nine broad-shouldered victims that day recalls another day less favourable to Paladin records. On that occasion our game was prepared below the South Downs, from the alluring sides of which, sculptured by giants, a breeze was blowing across the pitch. The Paladins were in full strength and well-nourished, and as they had the choice (R. is satisfactory with the spin of the coin) they went in to bat. A few minutes before they did so, a local baker's roundsman had hastily cast his bicycle into the hedge side and told the home captain that he would play. This last-moment decision was his recognised way, and his place was waiting for him. With the Downs behind him, a lusty young man with weather-tanned face and flame-touched mop of hair, he bowled. It was the sport of a giant, but a deadly accurate giant; and the wind was in the tale, and helped the ball to come curving in just at the dot. One alone of all the Paladins could do anything at all in reply to this swift co-ordination of the forces of nature, and even he was numbered among the all ten batsmen sent back to their troubled captain by the process. I have always thought that the giants in *Pilgrim's Progress* were misreported by Bunyan, who pretends that extreme strength must be ever conditioned by want of technique. But who can ever be sure in the game of cricket, or who will be the last of us to refer in speech or print to "the glorious uncertainty of the game"? Another summer in spite of the roarings of the political world took us into Sussex, and once again the Paladins found their old destroyer, full size, ball in hand, with the Downs behind him. But this time there was not a stir in the air, the sunlight was like a pool of clearest depth. And perhaps the fast bowler with the ruddy hair had departed from his custom and given notice that he would play in the match some days before. Whatever the explanation was, his electricity was off; the Paladins dealt with him as though he had never troubled them in their lives, and as though they had waited hungrily for the treat; at a vast rate they sent their score flying up, largely off his bowling,

"and all the hills echoed"

as this one's fifty, that one's century, was applauded all round the ground. I must add that the good-tempered bowler at tea time seemed as glad about all this as when he had our own applause in the hour of his greatness and our extinction. And there too let me not fail in gratitude to the true cricketers, who can so accept the run of the game for or against them, and who rejoice in observing the accomplishment and the mastery even when they themselves are for a time put in the shade by them. If some other affairs of this world could be contemplated with more of this courteous unselfishness, this devotion to an ideal object, it might be a happier place. And that is why, over my mantelpiece, a picture of Don Bradman out in the field shaking hands with the marvellous boy Hutton, who had just passed the Australian wonder's record Test Match score, shall stand there as long as I can see to it. People come in and think (sometimes with a sly dig) that it is a signal of my passion for cricket. It is, and it isn't.

So much has been written and said by very eminent minds against cricket that I confess a certain defensive attitude in myself when it happens to be my subject. No doubt like poetry or moonlight walks or selecting wines it calls for a select audience. But I cannot imagine any one's opinion or treatise against the game, or any of the epigrams, disturbing the tranquillity of W. L. K. to whom we owe the institution of our match beneath the Downs. It is true that he is master of a rapid wit and strategic debating which he could bring into battle with little fear of any anti-cricketer, but usually I conceive that he would not trouble his head that much. He is by nature numbered among the kings of cricket, not those I know whose scores and styles have

entered their names in the pleased memory of the public—
in less conspicuous teams he is a player of no ordinary
capacity—but those who without grasping for it hold sway
on the field and in all that appertains. And singularly
enough he did not find this out himself until he was arrived
at manhood. At length he saw, as missioned men do see
great truths, that he and cricket were made for one another.
Now one could never dream that he had not been a cricketer
of this degree of worship from his schooldays. The mind's
picture of him rises to quell all timidities and hunt all doubts
out of the bosoms of lesser beings. When we approach his
cricket ground, we see him there before us alone, mous-
tachioed, unbonnetted, erect, as one who would singe the
King of Spain's beard, striding up and down behind a small
roller; and though the sky (if it is one of those skies) slings
small shot of rain and hail at him, his view is that there will
be a cricket match and that there shall be a perfect pitch.
Even when he bowls and I have the luck to get hold of one
of his experiments before it can turn, I feel faintly guilty
and profane, as when the royal Ghost was struck at by the
soldiers of Elsinore:

> We do it wrong, being so majestical,
> To offer it the show of violence,
> For it is as the air invulnerable
> And our vain blows malicious mockery.

However, if he *will* risk those slow floaters, sometimes we
may find him mortal. I must think I did wrong not to have
raised an invocation to W. L. K. at the beginning of this
book, according to ancient literary ritual, so as to be made
quite invulnerable myself, and be raised by example and
benevolent power to "the highth of this great argument."

K. is not uninterested in the winning of the match, and
with the object of doing that he is prepared at every point.
Thus, he compiles a record of the performances against his
team, or teams (he is the best of pluralists) by all who meet

them. In his sight we are all worth study. If all his fore-knowledge and his statecraft, and as I have revealed if even his fast bowler do not seem to be leading to a victory, he is more than ever "majestical." He comes in to bat while ruin spreads around with a cheerful salutation to the fielding side, but it does not conceal the iron resolution within; the moment he plays the ball back to the bowler you know that he is having no nonsense about "a hopeless position" and the rest. He can make a bat appear a wall. His control of both ends may baffle any one. But should even his defiance yield to some trick of fate, or counterstroke wickedly worked out by some of those carefree Paladins over their pints the night before, he rises superior; and at the end of the day is found congratulating one opponent after another on the things that they have done,—how does he remember them all? The picture of him should be one of those, such as ancient painters of the biographies of saints and martyrs made, in which the eye passes without division from episode to episode. I was visioning him on the field of play when suddenly the scene became the end of a cold lunch in the long upper room of an inn, open windows adorning it with nature's summer colouring, and there he was towering above the company, at the top table, an orator. The speech from the first adjuration onwards was admirable, but it ended with a pearl of eloquence: "I have a surprise for you —I think you'll agree it's a surprise. To-day the drinks are on me." That's what both sides called captaincy.

V

Instead of Dingley Dell

AMONG the devices of man at different periods for being a sociable animal and taking the road in a jovial crew, —the well-fed pilgrimage of Chaucer's friends in memory of Thomas à Becket, the antiquarian outings of Samuel Pickwick and his disciples, the provincial jollities of the British Association and others—a cricket tour is modern and satisfactory. We all think we hope for Dingley Dell, but missing it even in the hop country now we are perfectly happy with what we find—indeed perhaps Dingley Dell would not suit us half as well as our actual resorts with all the usual comforts; and having established a headquarters where the date of the "facilities" is the date of the calendar we may discover at leisure and in just sufficient samples the rusticities of yesterday lingering about. We, who by the time we arrive at some hamlet are no longer only the Paladins but in report and expectation transformed into the might of Oxford University, *we* are the show piece, and must not stay over our ale or the shovelboard so long that the novelty is worn off. This is excellent; for this way we shall not come down to the monotony and the minor disputatiousness which infect even the sweetest of hamlets and thatchiest of little old inns. All is seen as in a picture by Wilkie or by Teniers—seen once, in vital freshness, the main sense and secret of the matter, the faces, the humours, the tastes, the speech, the beliefs and superstitions, the incidents. This is the living picturesque, and it does not thrive so well if we pursue it too long and exactingly and lose our accorded character as true travellers, and persons of consequence. Sometimes on the ground itself our hosts, with country cunning and strength (it must have been the second pint, of course) shatter our cricket for the day, but let it not be feared that such an untoward event will diminish our preconceived reputation. No; for it is the triumph of the village to have done such things to "Oxford University." We shall be just as formidable, I take it, and as great a cause of anxious preparation, next time we come.

Besides, going from place to place as cricket-players makes us feel as if it were an occupation as well as a sport. People in the country we have chosen do not upbraid us as idlers, but almost invariably give the impression that they accept us as one of God's several interesting works. The old lady in the hotel, alarmed as she appeared to be at first by the number of large (and small) men with bloated leather bags, pretty heavy footwear and incessant activity who suddenly crowded the writing-room and wanted to telephone and attracted the bottles of beer into the dining-room, was soothed when she was informed they were no worse than cricketers. Her husband, she said, with the tone of one to whom husbands are figures in the remote past, companionable as the old furniture or the arrival of the safety bicycle, used to be quite a character. So many days he went off to it. Indeed she soon made us give some punctual account of our doings, and might well have been elected a vice-president. The recollection of her reassurance about the Paladins brings after it another, not altogether unlike. I was a guest at a country house in Germany and had promised R. or rather had obeyed his order that I would not miss more than a day of the annual tour; now Frau G. in the kindness of her heart was apparently desirous that I should not cut my visit short but stay as long as might be and talk over books and men and the England of other days with her husband. But, with the fear of R. upon me, I tried to explain that I was not a free man and that I was under an obligation to go about the county of Sussex for the next week or so, playing cricket. Frau G., not unnaturally, frowned a little as she heard this idle excuse—she had at least understood my expression—but she pondered a moment and then asked me if I should be playing before das Publikum. Though I felt a slight scruple in calling the Paladins' usual little fringe of spectators the Public, I said yes; and at that my gentle hostess looked thorough approval.

It has been one of my private pleasures with the Paladins on pilgrimage that we have a match at Horsham—or if the match is abandoned owing to rain, I am still glad to have been once again setting foot on that ground. On this visit my thoughts are kept upon the cricket only with the greatest discipline, for in that place I have an adoration exceeding all that I have for this mystery of pastime. There from wooded knoll to knoll, from leaning spire to lime-tree avenue, a swift and beautiful phantom is my master, and I fear that there is not much intention on his part to join the players or tarry with the one or two who make the Public on this day. The magnetism of Shelley has compelled many a pilgrim into this corner of the south land, as into that foreign shore far south of it again; thanks to this cricket business I can sometimes find myself (dream it may be) with him once more when I had scarcely fancied the hour might be granted ever again in a busy life. Even as I crouch behind the wicket, disquieted at what will happen if by my inattentions as well as incompetences the best laid tricks of T. and C. S. C. are frustrated, I have a music welling and flowing within me—there are no words to it, or only few and simple ones: "Here Shelley lived." Looking one way from the ground I fall into dreams with the dreaming spire, which leans as though in very truth it were gently sinking to sleep; within, beneath it, are grouped the tablets of the Shelley family (epitaphs so laconic, so revealing); beyond it you discover the quiet street of cool exquisite houses where his kindred lived, and then all those good old shopping quarters and stores and craftsmen's establishments at which he as a boy often paid a call or a bill. The umpire has meanwhile called "Over ball," and next by change of ends I can look past the railway bridge, a foot bridge which does not disturb the scene of the ages before the railway, at the rising ground of Denne, with its wide-spreading boughs and its occasional shattered spiky oak worthy of Herne the Hunter, its long tracts of softest greensward, its rushy outskirts. The great house is in the solitude beyond that romantic veil, but my first memories of its silent, grey, enigmatic face enable me to see it still as the boy Shelley must have known it, catching the hint of things marvellous, as from the glooms of the park trees he is believed to have received something of his impression of nature's majesty and profundity, waiting to come through his later years in poetry of wonder, panoramatic in painting and dramatic in feeling. For after all his "spirit of solitude" found utterance long before he quitted England for the pine forests of Italy, and I hear him declaring from his first impressions, earlier than those of the gliding boat on the Thames even,—

"While yet a boy I sought for ghosts."

It has constantly puzzled me, who am the descendant of many Sussex men, that the biographers of Shelley pay so little regard to the fact that Shelley was a Sussex man, and, so turning aside, do not apply in his instance amid their critical conjectures the rule that poets live most on their youngest and least premeditated discoveries in the world about them.

It was not a tour with a band of cricketers, but a day's enjoyment of the county team's programme which first gave me a glimpse and a guess of another little town with a spire for ever shining at me at the end of all the highways and byways of my mortal journey. "We must have faiths if but for spires,"—so I remember a line in a poem by Kenneth Hare last read by me about twenty-five years ago; and that is how I have felt since my father took me to Chichester on a far summer morning. There is only one person known to me who quite equals my spire-passion, and with her in the secret the vision at the end of the road is even more aflower with celestial perfection than I knew it before. But in this, we agree richly—in this and in my present theme altogether: since her cricket field is as full of play and players and daydreams and associations as mine, and her constancy to the company of Shelley and the poetic England which they have given us is unexcelled. To William Collins of Chichester in special! to him, whose "gentle spirit" was not altogether unknown to me that cricket day of years ago when so many a carriage and brake and trap poured forth its cheerful sport-loving squires and farmers at the Priory ground; for when did I not thrill to the nobility of that war elegy:

> How sleep the Brave! who sink to rest
> By all their country's wishes blest?

But now we find our hearts returning more often to Collins's Sussex poem, his hymn to Evening. For it seems to be a poem essentially of his home and his life, with its suggestions of boyhood adventure, with our own southern glory of landscape coming into sight through the darkening hour:

> But if chill driving sleet or blustering rain
> Prevent my willing feet, be mine the hut
>   That from the mountain's side
>   Views wilds, and swelling floods,
> And hamlets brown, and dim-discover'd spires,
> And hears their simple bell, and marks o'er all
>   Thy dewy fingers draw
>   The gradual dusky veil.

This, you may urge, is far away from the theme of cricket, even of Sussex cricket; but, as Cordelia noticed when we last summoned up Collins to speak his *Ode to Evening* for our quiet time, even in that faery poetry the game is found not unworthy of a line.

C.C.

> While Spring shall pour his showers as oft he wont,
> And bathes thy breathing tresses, meekest Eve!
>> While Summer loves to sport
>> Amid the lingering light. . . .

They used to play so, the young and old from the forge and the shop and the threshing floor, at the foot of the steeple; and never was there a better wicket-keeper than that, or heartier fairer cricket—akin to so much that I was mentioning at the beginning of these little researches into the character of our land.

Not so very long ago (since this book is not intended to consist of antiquarian yearnings) my father and mother stopped on their walk to watch a village game on a green not far from Chichester, and were rewarded by seeing as he arrived at the fall of a wicket a figure who is more often found in books or talk than in the present scene. The blacksmith with his working clothes and leathern apron on was marching out from his shop to get his innings, and he looked as sturdy a smith as ever moistened his hands with spit; which he did with sublime vigour as he got his bat ready for huge blows at any ball in reach. I forget if his hammering was as successful here as in the glow of his fire. It might have missed in a literal sense, but in the world of the just reward it could not.

> "Take but degree away, untune that string,
> And mark what discord follows."

In the England I have known, and I am not ignorant how tiny a part I can have known, the sense of this has predominated. What the future may do to, for, against our harmony of life who will assure us? Perhaps "degree" will be taken away without all that harsh consequence. Yet in our country life hitherto, the much execrated principle of grades of society, walks of life has been maintained not by compulsion but by inclination, and the keeping up of distinctions and of separate worlds in little has been done not just by those at the supposed top but by those, quite as much, who accept fortune and know a thing or two at the other end of the scale. It is a reversible ladder. And here, once again, I must bless the powers and the chances of the English love of games, and notably those ubiquitous ones, cricket and football; for through them it is possible for many a companionship, many an intimate view of life as it is, to happen to those whose circumstances would otherwise have made it difficult to achieve them. A much more powerful voice than mine has said something more on this: "If the French *noblesse* had been capable of playing cricket with their peasants, their chateaux would never have been burnt." So G. M. Trevelyan, in *English Social History*.

VI

The Stranger was Admitted

INTRUDING into East Anglia, as one who did not know what bouts and stetches were, one who did not do what is called work in those parts (and their plain definition is not easily overthrown), one who had no share in the incessant mastering of nature on which their livelihood depended, I was not over confident of escaping very far from the class of "a stranger" and "a clerk" rhyming with Turk. There was kindliness and practical help from the moment that I first stood as a tenant at the new gate, but there was remoteness, as the case obviously stood. The villages about me were as secret in some ways as if they had been villages of China. And then it came about that someone heard of my being willing not only to hand over my little offering to the cricket and the football club but to turn out if there were a place vacant on Saturday afternoons. This was the talisman; and on this ground I was not a stranger from the very first Saturday among those sons of the soil. The exceedingly small population of the place made it difficult for them to manage a club, and they naturally liked to add even a particle to their strength and perhaps a new face and voice to their company. Besides, several of them had recently served with the infantry at the same period and in the same ungodly muck as I—and that bond has never quite failed where I have been. It was a blessing then for one like me to become through this matter of bat and ball, for the day at least, one of the village and perhaps of neighbouring villages as well. Even the geography of these straggling and charming places opened out. I had not played many times when in our own tussocky meadows the visitors' umpire, who was dressed in full gamekeeper's velveteens and who supervised the proceedings with a bat in his hand as in old paintings of the game, had a word with me while I was at the crease. "I can see you have handled a bat before," he said, with an effect of liking it as he might like a good bit of stacking or a handful of promising grain. Simple words, but as soon as they met my ears I perceived that my hopes were good; and the words went round, so that even on other fields as yet unknown to me I was not treated when we went there as myself unknown, and of an unrelated order of society.

Thus it was that Tom Matton of a village some seven miles away, a man of fame in a circle of that radius and rather more,[1] was not slow in inviting me to play for his team with the additional command not to hurry home afterwards; and I wish to-day that I had been able to take advantage of this opportunity more often. Tom was said to be getting on for sixty-five years old, but his cricket was not at all over, and to be complimented by him (from the side of his mouth) on one's play was in those rural matches to have arrived. One day he wanted me for a match in a town, against a side of some pretensions and taste in flannels. It had rained, it had blazed, and no one quite knew what the pitch was doing. Tom's first batsmen were unlucky, and I was feeling the burden of their fate when I went in; he soon joined me, I see him yet with his old flat green cap and ancient rubber-soled shoes, sizing up the bowling at once and giving me an unsmiling look of caution mixed with confidence. So on we went, and he pattered up and down the sloppy pitch with stoic forehead till he thought our side was well ahead, after which he would scarcely run on any account but preferred scoring in boundaries. We lived merrily, and afterwards he was satisfied, though he did not phrase it much. He did not let me depart that night

---

[1] Amos, who used to umpire for us regularly, told his little tale of the rustic who, being asked the time, would answer, "That's twelve o'clock, exact—rather more."

from his inn until he had made me a freeman of all its ways and insisted on the clients making me an honorary member, without the words; I heard a lot of things about that village which though I had rented a house there twenty years in the ordinary way would not have been imparted. But Tom had firmly decided that cricket had made for me a place in the private room, and his state was kingly (within fixed bounds) in that village. He bestowed upon me some general rules of conduct arising from the tales of gallantry and gain which were passing about while the chirrupers were "drinking in," and from him I learned something of the astute or the trusting manner in which the labourer regards or used to regard the great house and the lordling.

Yet in case this playing for another village than my own casts suspicion on me, I add at once that the gaudy days with shrewd old Tommy and his boys were exceptional, and that it was with the men of my own village that my best hours of understanding were achieved. Perhaps the unity came through football even more than cricket, for our feelings about the winter game were more intense, and the sense of a small devoted band was keener. From all points of view the affair was more of a fight, and we "came down to earth" all of us because our changing room was sometimes no more than a very windy cart hovel or the ditch by a gnarled copse; and when we had fought it out there was a most charming spirit of unanimity among us at the Live and Let Live or the Antelope. I do not mean that there was no critical mutual inquest! but the team that stood for the village of Staizley felt all together in one cause and nobody in it was excluded from its discussion and confession and odd knowledge. It did not matter then that I knew less than the sparrows of soils, seeds, implements, ailments of sheep or mole draining—I was given the run of it all. Adrian Bell (in the same county) earned all this by becoming a farmer and by being Adrian Bell; I did not get so far over into the private and ancient world of East Anglia, but by the short cut of which I write much was permitted me "to scan and learn."

How else should I have heard such songs, sentiment's ghost stories wandering along from the days of Cobden and Palmerston, as "You're going to leave the dear old home to-day, You're going away, You'll never see this cottage, boy, no more; So spake a loving mother Unto her only son, Who went afar from England's peaceful shore"? The feeling of it, as that prize scamp Ock, who when not "otherwise engaged" could shed tears of purest sorrow, delivered it in a much admired falsetto in the parlour hung with embrowned oleographs! Round went the pint pot at speed. But it was not only curiosities that village games brought me, or that they will bring to others. Those would have been of little lasting worth. I was given the candour of those whose lives had been sown and grown in hardship and insufficiency, but still had sprung up well in human liking, purpose and humour; their keen faces revealing many quick thoughts and feelings over pipes of shag are known to me, and they tell me their side of the modern age without anger or hesitation. If a man might do as much for life as they have done through the centuries, the "unskilled," the swede-bashers, the rheumatic masters of hill and dale through seedtime and harvest, he should lie easy at the last. They are the most modest of beings when you have them at leisure, attributing to you activities of uncharted difficulty, and corresponding accomplishment, and presenting their own (the result of ages of patient notice and consideration and physical courage) as a commonplace.

And still I cry, had I not had cricket and football, these characters and their country honour could scarcely have come within my range and into my deeper being. It may be a peculiarity of the English, but there it is; and once I was able to introduce an American friend, whose baseball style while it lasted was not displeasing to us, for one day of this traversing of a traditional ring fence. He is able to discover something like it on Elk Ridge. Glancing back to my East

Anglia, I am aware of having been on a cricket tour of a different kind from most; for it lasted some years, and among its members I was the only wanderer—the others were at home. The setting was constantly simple, with perhaps a stripling stream flowing between the area of the wickets and the holes and hills of the outfield, or a couple of willows and a cowpond just behind square leg. I still remember with incurable discontent the spoiling of my rare big hit by an intervening oak or a sweet cow who looked round from her study of grasses with mild surprise as the ball slapped her rich coat. But the game was good, for it was determined; the land was encountering the next land; there had been plenty of reasoned talk before the match, much curious comparison of players and methods. And out of those times come to me especially the forms of two tenant farmers and their sons, who all of them contrived their cricket and football seriously yet so as never for a moment to desert their wise labours. S., who rides the shaft horse to the watering-place for ever in my twilight picture, scattering the hens and ducks with outcry into the weeds, was a father who believed in his sons as friends and as pupils; and if I recall a little thing which his steady memory will have retained it is not for vanity. He was sure that whatever the art is, there is a right way and a wrong in it, and he observed that the defensive play which I had been brought up to use in batting was right. So of an evening, outside his farmhouse with the bees toiling in and out of the carved woodwork and the martins speeding with recaptured joy to and from their tenements in the eaves above, he would summon the boys; and I had been summoned too, with reference to a bit of supper and a look at the new horses. Young Willie with the sunny locks and cheeks like the winter sunset was particularly told to watch this locally uncommon art of cricket defence, where the ball might do anything at the last second. The boy did so, ignoring the occasions when his father's trust seemed to be betrayed by me, or perceiving that it was not the idea that was faulty but that I had recked not my own rede; and later on, when events had carried me out of the parish, I heard that even old S., was tolerably contented with the student's progress. The boy had quietly created such a defence as to make scores never dreamed of on our queer ground cut in the long grass —the power of hitting he possessed already; and the story is one that I may be pardoned for liking rather deeply, as signifying that for once I was able to contribute something to the leisure-hour life of a village that gave me infinitely more.

VII

Card of the Match

You arrive early, even earlier than you meant, on the scene, and you feel a little guilty at the thought of the day you propose to deliver up to sheer luxury; the printer's clacking machine in his little den is only just delivering the card of the match, and that, apart from "ads," is as yet only a register of names. You look down these names, and for a moment uncharitably wonder if after all you will go back to duty and profitable employment; for X and Y and Z are not playing, and the card foists upon you in place of these commodores several names of whom you have heard little or nothing. Still, after faintly recognising someone who used to be fairly regular on the Cannon Street train and is now putting hair off and weight on, you make for a place on the almost empty benches. You resolve dimly that you will make the best of the situation although the glory is departed; you even hope increasingly that the clouds will clear off; and meanwhile the bell has been rung in the pavilion where a few figures seem in no hurry at all, the roller and such impedimenta are being trundled off the ground at a good pace, and the two umpires make their sacerdotal entry. Not very long afterwards, you find that your solitary state has without much trouble quite vanished; you were lucky to take your seat so soon; and the chirrupings of the schoolboys and the elegant discernments of young men around you assist in banishing any illusion that big cricket is not what it was. The bowler is making his mark with his heel in the turf. Energy only waits the next second. "Play,"—and the music of the game begins, all new.

"That many-headed beast, the crowd," is of course what it was, and sometimes it makes you, in spite of its being composed of "you," cross. Its memory appears to be so short, its gratitude so fragile. At Brighton I was once amazed to find that Arthur Gilligan, who had only a little while before led England with great wisdom, dogged-ness and personal accomplishment in Australia, was being treated on his own ground as a kind of harmless passenger; he was batting late in the order, and under the effect of an injury. (Of the injury the spectators knew nothing then.) At Maidstone I was not less surprised when the fielding of those hop-county glories Ames and Valentine, surely not easy to equal, was being hooted at because of one or two brilliant attempts at the impossible which might on any other day have worked. On the other hand, the crowd is seldom unwilling to give plenty of merry encouragement to the unexpected man who comes from nowhere into the company of the masters and has a good day. He seems to represent the crowd, I take it. Nothing is relished more than the occasional success of the last man in, when he escapes a "Number Eleven decision" and wields the bat with cool style and the help of heaven. His name which just now was immaterial suddenly becomes as familiar as Hobbs and Hendren. I suppose one sees in this a variation on that most popular of all stories of ball games, David and Goliath.

My memory, as I have said elsewhere, is not enduring the wars of attrition unharmed, but it may not lead astray while the name of K. G. Macleod recurs to me from far away. I have not consulted the books, but I believe that he was for a time a player of some distinction; nevertheless when several boys, including me, sat among the boots of the multitude on the grass at Tonbridge, his name was certainly not at first among those which stirred the young cricketer's blood. But his innings did. It may not have been anywhere near the most productive recorded in score books on that day of summer scent and shower. He scored 63, as far as I know; a good total, but not itself immortal. Yet how he flashed into the scene, how like a romantic hero with a sword that could know no tarnish, no graceless flow! Our own Blythe was bowling at him, bowling rectangles as they used to say, asking a batsman to enjoy life with both hands —and sky one or another of these rectangles into the hands of Hardinge out on the edge of the boots of the multitude. But Mr. Macleod did not weigh the chances austerely. No doubt in the end that freedom mattered, and had to be accounted for. Before that regretted moment, he had made his impression on some of us for a lifetime; there was an over when thrice he drove the deadly thing like the most innocent ball we might ourselves bowl at first bounce among us. And tall and magical Blythe put his blue cap back a little from his forehead, as if to say, "I'm not quite sure that we have this gentleman placed as yet."

George Cox of Sussex, now succeeded by his son of the same name and like cricket ability, was reckoned a useful and plucky batsman in the later stages of an innings, but his forte was his bowling. Some even then said, Yes but you don't know his gardening; but of that I am no judge. On the golden day at Chichester in a peaceful year, to which I have alluded, some special grace fell upon the batsmanship of this sweet-spirited cricketer. Others did great things too, but he, as it were without warning, took the form and manner of a consummate stroke player, and I may not be far out in ascribing to him the result of 167 runs, not out. That does not in mere statement signify much. What does, is the emerging of this wonderful harmony of all the arts of batting; no one there (I heard them saying it) would have predicted it for George Cox that morning. The tone of his on-driving, the delicacy of his cutting, the inward judgment of the gaps in the field remain in my thought as a model of fine doing. Later on (a World War having come and gone in the interval and failed to upheave some pillars), he was to show similar form at Lord's, but it was in his proper surroundings that—as our neighbours on the benches said while they gathered their papers and tobacco pouches and their sense of time-tables at the close—he came out with "the innings of his life." And was C. B. Fry playing?

There is a complaint against the prevalent character of first-class cricket which many of us accept without much hesitation. "Cricket"—I trust that the quotation is at least more unfamiliar than the complaint—"is quite national, and, from early habit, I never come to London without visiting the ground at Mary-le-bone, where, indeed, though admiration is greatly excited by the perfection with which the game is executed, yet there is a feeling present, which, I think, rather checks the exhilarating remembrance of our earlier pleasures. The play there seems to partake too much of the cold character of science, and to have something of the insensibility and hardness of mechanism about it; and there is a cautious slowness in its progress which shows how much the wary understanding and how little the promptness of the heart is engaged." This dignified passage appeared in print so far back as 1835, the writer being the Rev. Charles Townsend, the delightful Curate of Preston in Sussex. Had he lived long enough to watch with me at least the early stages of an innings of 150 by J. W. Hearne, I suspect Mr. Townsend would have renewed to me the substance of his criticism in briefer terms. But he might soon enough have repented of it; for Hearne, if I remember, like other batsmen who elect to play cricket not as others would have them but as their natural powers fit them, suddenly retorted to the noisy part of his spectators by clouting two or three fours in a most indisciplined, rude and angry way, and then with a grin resumed the innings he was bent on shaping in *his* way.

Years have gathered already since we lost J. W. H. T. Douglas, who was there at Lord's one day when the skies were iron, and the pitch dough. I don't think very much depended on his staying there at the crease on that occasion, but to stay J. W. H. T. Douglas was resolved. The crowd, in mufflers and overcoats, thought that the last hour of play, if the word is not too amiable in this context, could and should be livened up; Mr. Douglas did not think so—at least he did not propose to enliven it according to popular principles. When somehow his bat lapsed into scoring a single, there was the customary offering of grim applause; but presently he allowed no more lapses. He was in fact treating us to a parody of the art he excelled in, "a cautious slowness," and by the drawing of stumps he had made nearly all of us see the inwardness of cricket with his eyes. The bowlers of course did their very best to tempt this St. Antony; offered him gifts, large, luxurious and enticing. The saint remained calm. The very last ball of the day had all the appearance of being due for a voyage into the highest storey of the pavilion; but the Essex captain treated it with a profound seriousness, played it as a fatal note, let it stop within a few inches of his bat, and then with a broad laugh of triumph marched away into the dressing-room. And while I follow that redoubtable figure in my retrospect, it occurs to me with a pang that the ball described was the last I ever saw Douglas repel. As Thomas Hardy says, "It came to an end"—but why, and why so secretly? This, however, is the happier dispensation.

This and that extraordinary innings by a single player probably should not haunt me, or would not if my sense of this great team game were perfect, as much as they do; and yet they may be counted as images of strength of purpose and superiority to adverse fortunes which I should be sorry to impute only to the spectator's creed of hero-worship. The cricket-speaking world must be full of people who recall one or another of R. E. S. Wyatt's delaying actions as a masterpiece of the kind. For me, when this question of the individual holding the fort arises, it is always a match at Lord's between the M.C.C. and the Australians; and M.C.C. are batting for the second time with nothing to hope for and a miserable pitch and entombment light to do it with; and Wyatt from the opening of the innings is resolved that he will not allow even Messrs. Grimmett and O'Reilly to get him out or the side out. And he did not. Somewhere towards the end there was a crisis, which even he must have felt as such: the seventh or eighth wicket went down and the remaining M.C.C. representatives were anything but batsmen in relation to the bowling of that hour. But "the arrangements were in the capable hands of" our Wyatt. The endeavours of our great opponents to outwit him at the end of each over when he was set on scoring a single or a three in order to keep the strike did not hold him. All the time he assailed every ball that was just a little less dangerous than the rest with willing and powerful enjoyment. And, everything working in obedience to Wyatt regulations, he saved the game and went happily to his own century just before the moment of the close.

While that feat is my topic, I cannot but revert to another, again with the confronted might of Australia as the chief condition. That time it was a tremendous struggle at Trent Bridge, and England had scored heavily, but heavily is never enough "against these Australians." E. Paynter, of Lancashire, was expressing his place of origin and views on nature and other cricketers in one of his Test Match soliloquies, an innings which had gone on for a long time, and we wished it to continue, for the runs were important. *He* and his bat were apparently beyond the spell of human bowlers, but what of the rest? He was joined by young Douglas Wright, who had only recently made his bow in county cricket, let alone international, and that exaltation had been on account of his bowling. This youth, who no doubt had his captain's orders, saw no reason why he should not stay and ensure that Paynter should have the fullest scope; as he had done on the corner of the green, he simply played the straight-bat game. Half an hour had gone by before he himself got away from the hated figure o, by means of a mild and eternally safe push towards deep mid-off, and the cheer that followed this single was loud and sweet. We almost forgot Paynter's double century.

All this brings me to what may remain for many years the most remarkable example of character shown in a cricket performance—the Test Match innings of young Hutton at the Oval ground in the dizzy August of 1938.

I believe that this patch of ground had witnessed, two centuries earlier, the fortitude of some political prisoners, sentenced to a public execution. But I should not easily credit that a greater nervous strain could be put upon a modern man than what a Test between England and Australia, at the later date, imposed. The thousand tongues of Fame and Rumour had cried up cricket on this scale until it was becoming an international crisis. Every particular was instantly reported or misreported through the extent of the Empire, and it may not be amiss to say that a contest between Australia and England is not precisely a sweet sentimental eclogue. It was my good luck to be among the throngs who saw at least part of the achievement of the youthful batsman Hutton, of Yorkshire.

As I read it, the debate lay essentially between him and W. J. O'Reilly, whose bowling begins so long before the ball leaves his hand. Australia breeds "demon bowlers," and he is of that lineage. Australia once produced poets who were English poets a little out of touch; now she has her own; and O'Reilly with ball in hand is quite the parallel of an Australian poet, territorially distinct in rhythm, passion, scheme and transition. Within him, an experience decidedly different from even the dales or the hills of Yorkshire is for ever prompting and proposing. On this day (the second of the match) he was not less formidable than usual, though in recognition of the difficulties of his task he looked (like the lovers in Thomson's *Seasons*, which probably he has taught his school classes) "unutterable things." The wicket was officially easy, over-prepared—yet we saw the ball bounce enough to escape the wicket-keeper's jump. All day O'Reilly was a menace, and all day Hutton played him as a perfect pupil, sedulous in his use of instructions—he has since had barely time, yet time enough, to advance beyond that stage. Report had it that in this Test Match he was directed all along by older cricketers, instructed in every point of subjection to his high calling, even to the devouring of a banana for his lunch, and it looked so; the fact diminishes his glory not a shade, indeed it makes it greater. Hardstaff and Leyland, as it appeared to me, met the occasion in a more majestic style as seasoned troops, but the English cause rested upon Hutton's immensely virtuous studentship.

The second day was one of clouds and darkness, and had the rains descended it would have surprised few. Play was delayed in the morning and cut short in the evening. Hutton walked into the pitch with a score of 160 and when he had increased it to 300 (a fantastic figure) the umpires accepted the conclusion, darkness, without a second's deliberation. The Australian plan appeared mainly to be packing the field on the offside in the hope that a spinner would some time lift up from Hutton's outstretched bat—caught. He parried that challenge, and he did not allow O'Reilly to bowl at him until the ball was actually in the air—all that hobgoblin work in the run-up discounted. The young batsman might have been writing a book on the art which he had acquired. All was performed so that C. B. Fry might have analysed all and gone home with classical satisfaction—"Omne tulit punctum." The batsman's body and his bat were as truly one as love itself. "Constancy to an ideal object" inspired the boy, and no doubt many young temptations to chance this or that piece of pyrotechnics were rejected with speed like light. "That would be just what I was told not to try."

Approaching the 300th run of his own innings, Hutton gave the impression of being accustomed to such a situation, and, as the London sky grew really sinister, he collected his runs without passion but thriftily, one here, one there; on his taking the 300th with a suitable little push (to say in such a prominent place just as in any old game that a run is a run whether 1st or 300th) the umpires instantly allowed an appeal against bad light and the day's play ceased. But not the innings. "Hutton—Continued," said the posters next day, and on the train to town I saw the engine driver escape from his post at one of the stops in order to snatch a glance at the latest news. It was just as he and the passengers wished—Hutton had set up a record in Test Match scoring; and in consequence of this immensely patient and serious yet charming innings—thirteen hours of temptation repelled—the match became an overwhelming victory for England.

"But man is not born for happiness," as Dr. Johnson pointed out so frequently, and the sequel to that victory was worth noting. I do not know if it is an illustration of the fickleness of popular sentiment or of the paradoxical nature of us Englishmen; certain it is that the victory soon assumed an aspect of inverted disaster. Scarcely greater shaking of heads and murmurings of dissatisfaction had been noticeable when our own team was being put through the mill in Australia. Something must be wrong! and even Hutton's innings was not quite so full-heartedly enjoyed in afterthought as it was at the time, while the collective achievement of W. R. Hammond's team was referred to rather as though it had been an illegal or discreditable business. And after all, it was a peculiar subject: the team with the greatest fieldsmen in the world (the Australian throwing alone is one of the sights of my time)—all this array to be reduced to impotency almost!. Meanwhile, the times were feverous; the world was at moral and nervous war preceding the actual war. Even so, that match at the Oval was the dominant English subject of that period, and debated with all serious minuteness.

And who knows if it ought not to have been? Many are the monitors who by pen and voice endeavour to call their countrymen, in days of peace, away from cricket and football and all other such dissipations. I do not know how in their thought they combine this jeremiad with their appreciation of Drake and his game of bowls. I am fairly certain, and the sequel to 1938 as a whole looks like sufficient evidence, that for the average Englishman this cricket and football and all the games and sports are the finest preparation for such military life as he may be suddenly required to lead. Mentally and physically they keep him young, when those of equal years elsewhere begin to age; and they help to nourish in him that religious simplicity which prevails no matter how empty the churches are; in the old words, each or almost each may say of himself (but he never would) that he

> Never was to fortune foeman,
> But gently took that which ungently came.

While I write, listening to the miracle of a paradoxical March that came in like a lamb and is struggling to go out like a lion, we are awaiting the succession of incidents in the war in Tunisia, where a British army called into being for a war only is vanquishing that of a most notable general. Let me rely on my friends at the front for the present truth of a not unfamiliar tradition: these Germans fighting in the desert are great soldiers. And yet the troops of Alexander and Montgomery are chasing them and getting them where we want them. The physical side of this extraordinary defeat of the highly trained by those who "looked in to oblige" is surely not overlooked by all the German observers; and those may think with me however ruefully that there is something after all in this matter of cricket, football and generally the Englishman's love of games. I will leave it to some future philosopher of theirs to probe into the other side, that of attitude to the variations of success and failure; for not the least striking thing in this North African War is the fact that our defeats did not at all defeat our temper. It is a priceless source of strength, this infallible "insouciance," and it has not been uninfluenced from those games where even mighty Hammond and Bradman sometimes find themselves walking back to the pavilion without a run, and smile as they go; and the million are of their way of thinking too.

VIII

The Heroes

IT IS possibly a less nerve-racking thing for the great cricketers to play their parts in the glare of the principal grounds, with all the circumstances of the contest of giants —the advertisements of Gin surely only attain their full size for Test Matches—than for such as me to watch them. They, after all, are on the whole meeting nothing that they are not prepared to meet; some are going to top the averages and some are going to have modest figures, but all are educated and versed in the same sort of cricket. The figures of the telegraph do not divide them into good, bad, indifferent players. They possess a general culture and insight "out in the middle," and such initiates may well be supposed to be at their ease even when we in the watching crowd number thirty thousand and make noise enough for twice that. But the serenity with which I have observed many a less celebrated yet regular player take his chance and enter the lists scarcely extends to me, his spectator. I can come away from a day's leisure as onlooker more exhausted (so I suspect) than the players, for I shall have been playing the whole of the day in every department with anxious imagination, and unrelieved sense of the difficulties of this final art of cricket. To this extent I may suppose myself in the line of William Hazlitt, though he sat at the edge of Old Lord's ground in a simpler mood, enjoying the ferocity and infallibility of the smacks to the boundary; but we know how the spectacle of the Indian jugglers caused him to feel. "To conceive of this effort of extraordinary dexterity distracts the imagination and makes admiration breathless. Yet it costs nothing to the performer" . . . Hazlitt's description shows that he was trying the work himself in his emotional fancy, with as much pain as pleasure, juggling indeed with his own nerves. But as for the feelings of the heroes of cricket, Hazlitt speaks, though it is of another game, in terms which are true here also, and wind themselves into the view of the Englishman's secret which I was just now dimly discovering: "It may be said that there are things of more importance than striking a ball against a wall— there are things, indeed, that make more noise and do as little good, such as making war and peace, making speeches and answering them, making verses and blotting them, making money and throwing it away. But the game of fives is what no one despises who has ever played at it. . . . He who takes to playing at fives is twice young. He feels neither the past nor future ' in the instant.' Debts, taxes, ' domestic treason, foreign levy, nothing can touch him further.' He has no other wish, no other thought, from the moment the game begins, but that of striking the ball, of placing it, of *making* it!"

The only Indian jugglers whom I have seen were such as had devoted their faculties for astonishing us slower ones to the magic of cricket. The first of these was by common consent the master magician—and "Ranji" was not past his best when I first saw him. It is not easy for a boy to distinguish the subtlety of the genius, and I felt in my ignorance that the leg-glide of this batsman could be copied by others; since then I have not seen it except once in an innings, so I expect that it was a piece of conjuring. So did the bowlers. This great gentleman returned to cricket after an interval away from his Sussex team, and as has happened more than once in our island story, he did so rather because he loved us than because he had any more ambitions for himself. He collected a double century, for example, and then knocked up a dolly catch; he showed himself in that action the same friend of the British as he was in statesmanship. I saw him once more. It was a bleak day of the Channel crossing temper, and even the pavilion at Lord's had about a fifth of the charm of the Reading Room (and

Karl Marx's ghost) at the British Museum. Swinging his legs and his stridently yellow boots from his perch on a long table, talking away to a set of younger cricketers whose faces I knew, there was Ranji. He was well aware of the game in progress, but was not watching every incident—he could take that in as though by some telepathic antennæ. His face was by this time that of wise age—or shall I say rather, of this old and travelled World?—and once he looked across his listeners and set eyes on me, almost as though he wished no one in the place to be or to feel "out of it." But I guessed that had he spoken to the stranger, he would not have talked directly of cricket. It might have provided an illustration. That look was beyond the cricket field.—My father bowled to Ranji in the nets fifty years ago, and was invited by him to try his luck in professional cricket.

I heard that this Prince was pleasantly displeased with his nephew, K. S. Duleepsinhji, for a rash action in a Test Match. The tale may have grown up from the fertile arable of good stories. The said rash action ended Duleep's innings at the total of only 173. "You should get your first hundred for the side, the next you get for the side, and then you may get one for yourself,"—such was said to be the old master's comment. It is true that Duleep on that occasion had become a little impetuous after some hours of absolute fidelity (in the blazing heat) to the principles of batsmanship. One Grimmett had been at him long enough. The English score was about four hundred, and the later batsmen did not look too good (but I never saw Somerset better represented than by Farmer White's thumping bat that evening.) So Duleep the sensitive began to lash out, and after some shots which scattered and enraptured the crowd, he was duly caught on the boundary; Blythe would have had him that way as well as Grimmett. He knew the story. We were all shocked a season or two later when it was announced that on medical advice the nephew of Ranji was obliged to pass from the game. He had been for several years the charmer, and when all is said and done, in cricket, in music, in painting, in poetry, in all the glories there are few who have the luck to be that.

The Nawab of Pataudi remained. To those who cling to some eighteenth-century principle that thrones and principalities mean shams and ignorances I would wish the felicity of an hour of conversation with him. I mean, listening to him. But this by the way. I seem to have been uncommonly prescient when I went to a day's play of the match between the ancient Universities in which he shone; at the time it had not been reported to me that he was outspokenly determined to shine. On the Cambridge side, A. Ratcliffe had run up the unprecedented score (for that series of matches) of 206—an innings which I am sorry to have missed, since it must have been the fruit of northern resolution above all. The tale I heard was that the Nawab of Pataudi had at once exclaimed that something must be done to correct this unbalance between Cam and Isis, and that he would do it. He went to work with a sedulous efficiency, as if he were more of a Chinese artist than an Indian and was preparing an extensive carved lacquer facade for a temple. The Australians found him similarly careful on large design and small points a little later. But this caution was drawn from decision rather than from personal preference. At last the witty and impish sprite began to play, and I recall some shots tickled very late past the wicket-keeper's claws and the slips which cannot have imparted "the humour of it" to them as they did to the Oxford faction. His score when he had produced a number of other prestidigitations all round was 238 not out.

For sheer obstinacy expressed in these terms, and if they are good enough for William Hazlitt they are good enough for me, I doubt if I can produce a better case than that of a bowler. It is fifteen years ago—and fifteen such years for me and all of us—but I easily revisit the Taunton ground for the purpose. Taunton! My grandfather married his lady from there, and of all that love and romance I have not a momentary vision. The generations go on and in turn we are all enclosed in our own ring of dated experiences; some feel that the day may come when all will be mutually revealed without the least difficulty. My grandfather, who took me in his arms as a baby, died at an age not much greater than mine now; I know him only by his portrait. Most friendly of men, most honest, most easy-going! And she, who scarcely outlived him, so young to the last, so naturally electing the course that looked more arduous—it was probably on the Taunton ground that they first inter-locked fingers and planned as in a Hardy novel the home that did come. For Edmund Blunden—his name is hidden under the moss, except when I get my knife out to scrape and find him once more, in Allington churchyard—was a cricketer. He had a way of stepping in to the bowling, perhaps not orthodox then, but made so not long afterwards by George Gunn; and he enjoyed whatever came of it— and something came when his eye was in. Then again, *his* grandfather I imagine it was who makes an appearance about the time of the Retreat from Moscow in the score-book of the Brighton Brunswick club. A tragic, as a majestic title, if we look into it closely.

But all this is impeding my reader who was eager (in that case, dear reader) to hear of my exceedingly obstinate bowler. He was Robson, of Somerset. Once again, those terrific Australians were the adversary, and, in this respect they were adversary enough for one round world. Bridges, an old companion of my father in the cricket field, did well; but it was the veteran Robson who pegged away on true farming principles. I forget how his precise results stood at the end of that day, but the Australians had had to play to him all day long. His "useful" action slowed them down, and it looked as if he could have done his work in his Sunday suit and Trilby, so steady and mature it all was. The oppo-nent who chiefly affected the state of the game was one not unlike himself in that manner. Surely no one has ever paid the just tribute of prose or rhyme to Warwick Arm-strong. His practical irony has eclipsed his technical greatness. We read of him as one who pointed out to England, at a moment when we were apprehending no such set back, the laws of the game, overlooked by umpires of endless age. We see him posting himself—a stately landmark—at the greatest distance from the wickets, enjoying a fragment of the home edition blown to him by a gust of wind as dry as his own humour; all to express, in laconic sort, his opinion on the right and wrong way to play cricket, even if it were Test Match cricket. But, that day in Somerset, I departed with the enduring impression that W. W. Armstrong was one of the supreme executants of his game. He made a bat look like a tea-spoon, and the bowling weak tea; he turned it about idly, jovially, musingly. Still, he had but to wield the bat—a little wristwork—and the field paced after the ball in vain. It was almost too easy. W. W. Armstrong sat down while they fetched the ball. If I were to write a Dictionary of Cricket, I would enter in the Index: Armstrong, W. W., *see* Grace, W. G., and Grace, W. G., *see* Armstrong, W. W.; and it might not be forgotten in the text that Armstrong could bowl—ever so easily, ever so amiably. . . .

They vanish, these immortal players, and we suddenly realise with astonishment that years have passed since we heard a passing mention of some of them. At one point they seem as much a part of the permanent scheme of things as the sun which glows upon their familiar faces and attitudes and the grass which makes the background for their portrait; and then, bless us, it is time for even them to go. Great cricket has its merciless side. They go while still they are far from being old men, and their crowded honours are swiftly obscured in the rapid growth of new names, new methods. In life outside the cricket world they may or may not be successful; but their meaning is surely almost lost, as that of Ovid was when he was exiled among the barbarians.—It is pleasant to be of some use to the spirit of someone who has outlived his chief life. On the bus-top the other night, a thin-faced and mild-mannered passenger began talking to me. A chance allusion to the shortage of matches and of cricket matches drew him out, and he said that he had formerly been a first-class football player, and taken part in many celebrated clashes. He enumerated the chief, but in his voice I detected no note of vanity; it was rather the voice of a puzzled soul. So few years ago, and he was in the centre of all that, and after one mighty action another followed, and there was always to-morrow, or next Wednesday; and now, and now there never was. O yes, he was getting a living, and so far he did not dislike the life of a village; but there was an inner darkness where, only just now, there had been sparkling lights galore. I said as I descended that I hoped we should meet again, and he assented to that; for perhaps his neighbours did not manage to let him turn on the lights of the gallant past very often. The Football Pool has flowed with turbid haste over interest in the men who played so lately, the manner in which they played.

And Fame is still as fleeting, as false, as nonsensical as in any of the ancient authors and moralists; as nothing-doing as in that woodcut of wonderful Thomas Bewick, wherein against the fractured column inscribed in deep perdurable lettering to the glory of some great victory—but which great victory?—the ass comforts his hind quarters as he rubs his sore hide. "Keats—what are Keats?" was an honest and a representative question. I asked old Harry Dale, the factotum at my house at school, who came every day from Broadbridge Heath, whether he had anything to tell me of one Shelley, a former inhabitant. He had. First, there was the Shelley Arms, which certainly he mentioned with a tone of faith and hope. Well, then—yes, Shelley; he had heard a thing which he seemed a little unwilling to reveal. "Used a young boy something cruel he did. Beat him to death." This may yet have had some faint relevance to the angers of Bysshe and even Timothy, those mighty landowners preceding the kind spirit Percy; and of course Harry did not know of the Theses on Shelley which have been compiled in every language under heaven. Still, the quality of the meagre legend cast a shade over my young mind, given to believing that genius triumphs over time. I do not know if the assertion is still true, but not so long since I heard that among all the ships of the Royal Navy not one bore the name of Blake. The marvel of Duns Scotus has long vanished into a name for harmless fools, and Peter the Great, that daring rebuilder, has had to resign his title to a city and an empire.

There are worse ways of occupying leisure than tours on foot through noteworthy cemeteries, so long as one does not overstay one's welcome. The two sides of the matter—the startling efforts of some to wrest from nature a personal glory that never was, the quiet relapse into the shade of others who once in fact attained it—make up a dramatic scene. SISTE, VIATOR! And unless my sense of the tendency of men's feelings is all wrong, Fame no longer moves the spirit as once she did. This religion like some others has fallen into a decline. Better a living dog than a dead lion; and modern lions may have to go begging for the remains of lunch from the touring car. Wilfred Owen perhaps was the latest English poet to meditate on Fame with a glimmering of the same feeling as burns in the Elizabethans. He would by now have deserted the goddess, in favour of the joy or the tumult of living in the present. Yet one day Fame will arise anew, will reign for a season in her old manner; and her triumphal works during that season will in turn become the setting for the zest and bustle and passion of those who will care nothing for her.

IX

Men and Moments

I WILL yield to the temptation to say a word still on men famous in the cricket world of my time. Perhaps brevity of allusion best befits an onlooker. Of Harold Larwood, whose cricket life bewildered, even embroiled the multitudes in Britain and Australia, I chiefly recall something too slight to have been recorded in the press. I was going into the Oval ground, and as I went I was raising my head to spy over the hats of the front rows of spectators; and I saw the most terrifying fast ball wing down that I had seen. It did nothing; it was a full toss. But the authorship even to my eye was unique. I had seen, if I saw nothing more by that hand, the best fast bowler of the day. Don Bradman has made so much cricket history of the marvellous sort that one scarcely ventures to speak of him; but in a Test on the ground just referred to, he brought off a shot which no doubt was to him just one of a thousand like it. A fast ball was bounced at him, head high; he had not come to the crease more than five minutes before, but he swung his body and bat as if stung to anger, and the ball went flying almost straight behind him like a cannon-ball into the crowd. A. P. F. Chapman was fielding deep on the off side, to Tate's bowling, at Lord's. Bradman's score was 254, the sunshine was such as conspires with batsmen and not bowlers, and he meant to go well beyond that 254. He drove one of Tate's accurate-length balls as before, but the hit was a little off the ground; Chapman was sensitive to this from the start, and with a long right arm, he collected the hit at a few inches from the floor and Don Bradman was out. I could not have dreamed of this, nor could most of us, but it was done. Chapman mopped his forehead. At

Manchester, when the Australian innings was hardening inexorably, Woodfull's partner played the ball well down past Hammond in the slips—a safe run. Hammond moved, gathered, turned and flung and Woodfull, spying danger and making a vast attempt to get home, was out. Nobody in that learned cricket crowd seemed less bewildered than I or very possibly than the batsman. Hammond appeared to have cancelled the duration of time. These are but commas in the careers of the players mentioned, but they linger written on a spectator's brain. Greatness can be identified, like the touch of a painter, in a detail. Prescience is worth seeing in a sceptical world.

Of Hobbs, the well-graced I particularly retain a very simple impression, but it has outlived all the others; it was his ability to make the lightning delivery appear to be in no hurry at all, so far as he and his bat were concerned. There was no fast bowling to that immense clarity. E. Macdonald, in one match, came to this conclusion, and acted on it. It was a pity, for Macdonald bowling fast was good to look upon. Of Hendren, whose powerful refusal to take any situation for lost we shall not all forget, I hold one memory in special, and yet it does not touch his great days, any more than Mr. John Betjeman's rhyming his name (not at all irreverently) with "rhododendron." It was his adieu to the cricket in which he had from east to west been so general a favourite. He played his little innings of nimble neat shots, just had time for one of his old mighty bangs to the railings, was then bowled with not the slightest doubt in the world, turned at once to go with a shake of the bat at the shattered stumps—and having paced away gaily twenty or thirty yards stopped, looked back rather sadly, waved them all a good-bye. The humorist this once had not the leading part in an action on the green by Hendren.

C. F. Walters never made a century in a Test Match against Australia. A score of 82 at Lord's had in its progress shown every sign of becoming one. It was the most flowing, well-tuned, elegant innings that I saw in those formidable games; the happy discernment and advancing originality of the artist were smiling through it all. And yet it is the end of that composition which haunts me. The batsman played a ball that popped on the leg side a little off the ground, and that little air was enough for A'Beckett (I think it was he) to make a conjurer's catch. Walters, standing at his block, saw this as one witnessing event in detachment, and in the most thoughtful manner he played his stroke again before he left the wicket; the experience presumably would lead to still finer control and selection next time, and the question of a century would be solved accordingly. But it would not be the essential question.

And these notings must cease, and I am alarmed a little that I have been letting them take their course so far. One of the crowd, and not of the most regular or sharp-eyed either, how should I be entitled to any impressions at all on these leaders of the subtlest game in the world, or to conjectures on their motives, their distinguishing qualities? Yet according to the tradition of judges and umpires, I may trust to the benefit of the doubt, and all the more because these little memoranda represent at all events a tried devotion. Not wholly altered from what I was in boyhood, I still find in the master cricketers and the intense and never forecastable competitions between them an apparition of the heroic. Better thus, than in the ancient style. A classical scholar of my acquaintance, who has been if he is not now among the names that count in his field of studies throughout Europe, often tells me that he has ceased to find much pleasure in the poems of Homer; he cannot now endure the cataloguing of heroic carnage in those hexameters. "And the beauty of the matter was, that the world was no sooner conquered by one hero than it wanted conquering again by another." This beauty at least continues as an ever prospective force in our cricket, but the world which is conquered there is that of care and dull reality and the strain and dry urgency of the cities; or it is the region of Technique, a god who lends some redeeming virtue to every mortal occupation, and made the child-like De Quincey write a paper on Murder. Cricket will serve us as chivalry, though its armour is limited and simple, and only Hendren ever sped forth into its lists with the addition of a helmet, seemingly supplied from his own comic workshops.

That innovation was not intended otherwise than as a protest against innovation; and though cricket undergoes its changes the affections rest upon its continuity. Why should we resent the inclination of man to possess some central point, some home and haven, to which he may come back at last and not feel estranged?

> So we'll go no more a-roving
> So late into the night. . . .

Even Byron, in *Don Juan*, is thought to have been uttering a curve of experiences, circling back at last so far as he could see into the England where he too had played cricket. It was not his principal recreation. But it was part of the appeal which was hovering over him at the age of thirty-six: part of the country life which after all he depicted from the distance to which changefulness had taken him in colours as fresh and in tracery as precise as if he had been walking among his old lawns and lily-ponds and Gothic arches. Byron at Lord's would have been a disconcerting presence to some of the other patrons, but not to the spirit of the place.

Yes, cricket changes—the great matches I should say more than our local attempts. In my father's boyhood, the county player was not the dedicated being that he now is, but the same man to whom, in the evening after he had been serving up his donkey-drops on the big ground, you took your shoes to be cobbled. Though I had no such domestic contacts with these performers I am reminded of a sunny day when I resolved to enter a shop and purchase, with the end of my resources, a clever and inexpensive book called *Who's Who in Cricket*. A mild little man with sandy hair came from among the racks of bats and pads, laid the item in my hands and told me I was doing the right thing. He took the book back for a moment, and through his glasses examined an entry or two, and I thought that it was almost reluctantly he went off to help another and surely more affluent customer. Afterwards I perceived that I had been waited upon by Bobby Abel, whose top score for Surrey on the neighbouring ground was something like 357—and that is still reckoned a bag of runs, from China to Peru.

The old days, the days that were sunlit, before mine, lacked a formal boundary. A big hit frequently forced the fieldsman to hurl himself among the legs of the spectators, some of whom were quadrupeds. But then the batsmen had to run out their runs. We know the hit for four, to the railings or the ropes or such a definite circumference, and the saving of effort which it makes on both sides. Games on sound wickets naturally go on longer, and an art of economic boundary hits has grown up. I believe too that to hit a six formerly, you had to strike the ball quite out of the ground; these degenerate days require no more than that it should soar over the ropes, which run well within the total space. Pampered moderns ! But is there much in the effects? One of the last games before the War, bits of which I saw at Oxford over the heads of a swarm of newly hatched priests—the Churches have ever regarded cricket-watching as a venial sin if it is any—was marked by a disorderly deed on the part of Perks, a bowler of merit. He does not usually bat for long. This tall young man arriving at the end of the innings made one or two awkward passes at the bowling and then he connected; and up went the ball, to scare a pigeon somewhere on the roof of the pavilion. The bowler put more pace on the next, but Perks saw it all the way, and it went aerially a bit farther. When it came back, and that took time, our representative tried his yorker on the leg stump, but that seemed merely to solace and allure the batsman, and the ball not only went out of the ground, but

almost out of the Parks and out of business. These three
sixes might have satisfied the examiners in 1880; or our
dear old connoisseur of cricket, cities, literature, anecdote,
personality, and indeed all this floating world, E. V. Lucas.
I have seldom been more apprehensive for a celebrated man
than when at the after-stage of a dinner given by a club in
town he was called upon for what he had the utmost misery
in supplying—a speech. In a solemn style he got himself
to the back of his chair, nervously extracted a bit of paper
from his pocket, and slowly recited four lines of verse from
it. Despite the sinking tones in which he read, the last
words proved to be of an "uplift" nature:

And a sixer climbs the sky.

To continue, the Press has done much to make the game
in its major form more of a total warfare than it used to
be. I confess I rather like the excitement and the eloquence.
The evening paper during a Test Match is apt to provide
us with three several accounts of the play. They fill most
of the issue. And not content with that, there are some who
listen to the radio descriptions! Well, I may be condemned
to some penalty in the underworld for my infirmity, but I
cannot help considering all these; I sometimes dwell on
the variants in the narratives as fondly as an editor of
Shakespeare deciding whether Hamlet said that he wished
his too solid, his sullied, his sallied, or souléd flesh would
melt. If only time would run forward merrily, and set this
body again in Rupert's little car—that rural vehicle, pulled
along not by petrol alone but by an abstractional nanny-
goat—among the woods of the Thames valley, while with
loud beating hearts we listened to the latest facts of the duel
between Edrich or Compton and Nupen or Mitchell! But
it may not be beyond hope. As for the newspapers, there
will be no crashing Letter to the Editor from me when old
Time reverting to holiday mood exchanges the issue of
essays on the bomb-psychology of the Italian or the German

public, or the tiff between the agricultural optimists and the Government department, or the superior vitamination of sawdust steaks over the butcher's variety, for one ridiculous plump gazette containing C. B. Fry, P. G. H. Fender, Bruce Harris, Anon and Stop Press on the current fixture at Adelaide. But, all the same, as Charles Lamb observed, "No one ever put down a newspaper without a feeling of disappointment."

And does cricket change? Add to all the above all you will of modified rules, of improved equipment, of the horrid ingenuity of groundsmen, of the universal circulation of the best principles as understood by the readers of the averages; add the quickening of our nervous demands; and still cricket is not so vastly other than when I first wonderingly accompanied my father to its healthy feast. On with the dance! Dance it is, and I fancy in naming it so I may be in the school of C. B. Fry himself, whom I cannot forget as he once led the way in the full radiance of the poetry of forward play and unified motion. It is one of the most stately of all dances, and a seventeenth-century poet might have proved it to be not less related to Nature's great round than the ancient Grecian theatre, or Gratiana "beating the happy pavement." Among those whom I have caught sight of, quietly revering it, regard for his shyness keeps me from naming the most perfect student, the most poetic seer of the Grecian form whom this century has anywhere produced. To him, if one may interpret his watching face, those white-clad figures in shining constellation about the axis of the two wickets are as the effigies on the friezes, or vases, of his lifelong remodelling. Lovers of the poetry of Keats must not dismiss me as unworthy of further association with them if I say of the cricket of my time that its groups and postures and borders are not unimaginable as pictures on another Grecian Urn such as he contemplated; or else I will attempt to convince them when the passing cloud of war leaves our greensward as golden as it used to be—sometimes.

> "A leaf-fringed legend haunts about its shape
>   Of deities or mortals or of both."

The cloud of war is passing. May comes in and the hedges are white-clad; the cows sit munching and staring at the first matches still coming to life by the white walls of the villages; this year at last there seems a dispersed feeling that the game may be played and talked over without ghostliness. It was a Yorkshire corporal who told me with a voice of conviction, while he tapped a malevolent wicket almost affectionately as though it created a dream of home, that Sutcliffe will be playing again in the days to come. Hutton too—but that was not in doubt. Sutcliffe is now a cricketer of unknown antiquity—let no one worry me with dates—who has never been a beat behind the newest geniuses, and whose proceeding on his handsome way after his second world war will quite cancel that interruption in an agreeable culture. I see him in the days to come holding the game together; the light will travel from his serene presence on one ground to all of them. This invincible man now represents his partner Hobbs as well—at least, when once again he seats himself on his bat after sweetly delaying to complete his fifty, the imagination will also perceive Hobbs at the other end reflectively twirling his bat or sounding the marl with it, as once upon a time. The inquirer into myths and what underlies them may tell us how such complete understanding is created as ruled the hour when these two ran their sharp runs. It is expressible in the terms of Shakespeare's enigma of the Phoenix and the Turtle:

> Single nature's double name
> Neither two nor one was called.

It might be worth considering whether the official score should not record these adunations of cricketers as single effects, under some shared name (on the analogy of the two poetesses who wrote in identity as Michael Field.)

Gregory and Macdonald, Hirst and Rhodes, Makepeace and Hallows, Fry and Vine, Larwood and Voce—are these couples not much more, or at least more potent and executive, than the addition of the individuals exerting their powers independently? What was Gilbert, what was Sullivan after that unholy little quarrel over the carpet in the office? which, like the ancient cataclysm said to have severed Dover from Calais, left these inseparables

Standing apart, the scars remaining:
A dreary sea now flows between.

Sutcliffe, great and good, like Queen Victoria in the song, will revive in the grey-headed and instil in the young all that his gallant companions have given to the fields of summer—he will perhaps give the boys the autographs of those whose glories shine entwined among his own. But then, there may be in the reconstituted game an edict against autograph ambushes, or rather commandos. It is time to re-educate youth. On the green, the cricketers are above mortality—

The leaders are fairest
But all are divine;

and are they to be waylaid with stubs of pencil and little books where bibulous Uncle Josh has drawn his seaside joke and clever Cousin Doreen has illustrated the advice "Don't be wet" with a pink duck hoisting an umbrella? No: but when Mr. C. I. J. Smith recites his selection from *The Lay of the Last Minstrel*, or Mr. ("Tich") Cornford lectures on "Ruskin's Brighton Period," then let them be treated as authors and duly reduced to autograph-yielding substrata.

The author who will take for his province The Cricket Spectator has, I believe, yet to appear. Balzac sought his subjects on the wrong side of the Channel. The onlooker at the great matches is not always so comprehensible as one might have supposed. I must mention one gentleman who, on a change of bowling which relieved Kent's wizard and gave Todd the ball, loudly informed all in range that Freeman was at length going on, and as for A. P. Freeman he explained with generous pleasure that "We call him Bill, you know, his real name's not Bill, it's Ernest, but down here we call him Bill." This private information tangled the audience up and no comment could be offered, but we wondered why this informative man had come to a county match. Especially as he spent the rest of the time, when not spreading his strange tidings, digging into a sort of carpet bag for food. "Used to play for the Professor's team, ha, that was before *your* time—Professor W. A. G. Grace's side —him and Gilligan—the *Rev.* Theophilus Gilligan,"—a swig of tea and a doughnut.

Alas and alas, too many of us in the crowd on all occasions are not so unlike this warm-hearted but inexact personage. I blush a little as I extract him from the past, for he is recognisable; with very little question he is me. Sitting by him, I make my comments and criticisms on every ball bowled, every stroke played, every tactical move; but to speak truth it is all seen in a glass darkly. We love to sun ourselves in fancy "out in the middle," but it looks and it is different out there. The fable extends its application beyond cricket, and I need not dwell on its meaning where, for example, "the conduct of the Allies" is being discussed with vehemence over the customary foam. But some of us have been rash enough to write biographies of eminent men who died before we were born, and whose voices we never once heard. Heavens, how did we venture that far? And human nature being what it is we may again. They will forgive us in any Elysian Fields there may be, or they may have been quietly

ignoring all that haps beneath the moon.

But I am uncomfortably suspicious that when we were

writing out our plausible and (so we heard) our readable version of their difficult conditions, their intellectual or domestic experiences, feelings in grief or conquest, we were really saying, "We call him Bill, you know, his real name's not Shakespeare but down here they like to call him Actor Bill—used to do a bit of pelmanism on the stage, previous to the old Britannia being sold,"—and the play goes on.

X

Our Authors: An Opening Pair

COMPLETE editions of Mary Russell Mitford's principal work *Our Village*, which passed its centenary a few years ago, are not easy to get, and no doubt the difficulty is one which agitates very few people. It does not agitate me; for a good genius showed me all the five volumes on a stall one day, and I did not decline the offer. Dr. Johnson observed once that he should like to read everything that Ogden had ever written, and without disrespect to Ogden and I suppose sound divinity I transfer this affectionate piece of dreaming to my voluminous Miss Mitford. Not that I would expect any one to agree with me, or indeed put forward my own remark as being more than a blissful visionary aspiring thing. It is possible that I have not yet really read those numerous volumes of letters in which Miss Mitford so warmly, so youthfully enjoys her literary world to the last. Any one letter would be as good as any other. Even the five valued volumes of *Our Village* embosom much of scene and episode with which, as it happens, I have still to establish real contact. But the bloom of the whole Mitfordian parish, the sounds and sweet airs therein, come over me not less for this incomplete pervagation. "Nothing," she wrote, "is so delightful as to sit down in a country village in one of Miss Austen's delicious novels, quite sure before we leave it to become intimate with every spot and every person it contains; or to ramble with Mr. White over his own parish of Selborne, and form a friendship with the fields and coppices, as well as with the birds, mice, and squirrels who inhabit there." Matching those personalities of country life in England I find her own, congenial yet not to be confused with theirs.

Through my study window the evening sky is a soft blue, scarfed with pink clouds, floating in a very sentimental manner—their colour is not modern, I understand; they may have been tinted by Miss Mitford, delegated for angelical duties. They might be the embodiment of the presentation leaf of some Book of Beauty which she is editing for the aristocrat subscribers up there. Certainly these rosettes and their ground of harebell blue are sweetly pretty: and such is the sense of her pages as I let them pass before a not too strenuous eye.

But it is not on account of this floral-aerial tint of spirit that I am now calling for a friend or two to look into the sketch-books of Miss Mitford. The same sort of general grace might be adduced as reason for talking of Mrs. Browning, or Miss Yonge, or even Mrs. Charlotte Smith —and these casual reflections would little by little become almost a history of women in English literature. But Mary Russell Mitford is not a digression, she is right in the line of march, she is the most cricket-spirited person in all my book. Would she have attended the matches which began to be played a hundred years after her day between the women of England and those of Australia? This I cannot decide; but she loved the game, long before it was the game for women, with a peculiar delight and a detailed knowledge.

Right at the start of her five volumes, this passion expresses itself; we come out upon the common ablaze with the gold of the setting sun, and there in the painting is her cricket match and the spectators—"But," she declares, "cricketers and country boys are too important persons in our village to be talked of merely as figures in the landscape." A little farther on, if we follow by the path she treads so joyously, and there comes a young man to watch a cricket match, but he forgets to watch it because his glance rests on one Hannah and he falls in love at once. But we still traverse many flowery meadows before Miss Mitford fully discloses her characteristic, her own distinction among our women writers, in that finished piece of narrative, *A*

Country Cricket Match. In that too the game has its halo of romance, or Cupid's quiver, and one James Brown is only induced to take part because Mary Allen, who has previously treated him coldly, is afraid that "we shall lose without you" and writes him a letter accordingly.

Miss Mitford sets out to discourse on a "Hard Summer," and as a naturalist she knows all about summer and about every season; but what happens? The cricketers steal the picture. There is her hero Joe Kirby who comes off work at seven "to work still harder, under the name of play—batting, bowling, and fielding, as if for life, filling the place of four boys; being, at a pinch, a whole eleven"; and there is Joe's rival Jem Eusden, who "still quarrels and brawls as if he had a faction to back him, and thinks nothing of contending with both sides, the ins and the outs, secure of out-talking the whole field. He has been squabbling these ten minutes, and is just marching off now with his own bat (he has never deigned to use one of Joe's) in his hand." Presently Miss Mitford goes on a visit, and what she finds is all a thing for us to dream of in these days, such quietude, such peaceful occupations, such sweet formality; but as she makes the journey, it must in the Mitford universe be arranged that "There, too, to the left, is my cricket-ground (Cowper's common wanted that finishing grace;) and there stands one solitary urchin, as if in contemplation of its past and future glories; for, alas! cricket is over for the season."

Still, all her worship of the mystery is summed up in a story with the unimprovable title, *Lost and Won*, and this downright opening:

"' Nay, but my dear Letty——'

"' Don't dear Letty me, Mr. Paul Holton. Have not the East Woodhay eleven beaten the Hazelby eleven for the first time in the memory of man? and is it not entirely your fault? Answer me that, sir!'"

Letty has no intention of letting him answer, even if he

knew how; and, to tell the truth according to her, her lover's record was black, or at best subfusc. He had pushed his way into the side, then got a duck in each innings, and dropped three catches including an absolute gift from a gentleman who went on to score 45. After these references, not unnaturally, the lovers are seen angrily separating "at a smart pace, and the one went westward and the other eastward-ho." Wherever he drew up, Paul did not write, and Letty was languishing. Three years elapse. "The Hazelby Eleven again encounter their ancient antagonists, the men of East Woodhay." Letty's father coaxes her to come and watch, enigmatically mentioning that Hazelby will have the assistance of a player "who practises the new Sussex bowling." It is (could you guess?) Paul Holton! Down go the wickets of the East Woodhay men, not one run is scored from the new-style bowling of Paul; and then when Hazelby bat, though he starts a little shakily, Paul slashes up 55 not out. Then he again bowls out the wretched East Woodhayites. "My dear Letty!" Never were wedding-bells so clearly predictable as on this occasion. Hark, how they ring!

The fervour of Miss Mitford for flowers and cricket is one and the same; her heart overflows with joy that such things are; they happen, they abound, and all's right with the world. This is a feeling which I can understand, but it is rare in our best literature, and women [1] have seldom gone farther than to regard cricket as the harmless squandering of summer days by their menfolk. Is there no place on the pavilion walls at Lord's, among all the pictures congregated there in happy years, for the portrait of this unique devotee? She should not be excluded because she objected to Lord's as the home of cricket played for money (town cricket meant betting in those days); but, if her likeness may not be canonised there, at least let a cricketer now and then even

[1] It has been a tradition, however, that a woman invented the round-arm bowling which Letty's father attributed to the Sussex players. My sister Lottie tried it on me later on.

in the grimness of one of our twentieth-century matches with the loud speakers vibrating in the southern hemisphere, all about it, remember that a woman in the eighteen-twenties wrote, "Who would think that a little bit of leather and two pieces of wood had such a delightful and delighting power?"

Before this lady wrote, what had we in the way of cricket interpretation? Mock-heroic, little else, and those who want it can have it:

> This now full well did Kent perform
>   After, on Sevenoak Vine;
> With six not in, the game was won,
>   Though White got fifty-nine:
> For Miller, Wood and Dorset then
>   Display'd their wonted skill:
> Thus ended the fam'd match of Bourn,
>   Won by Earl Tankerville.

I am quoting, I know, a very valuable and very rare piece, considered as an item in cricket bibliography, for a sight of which I am indebted to that admirable player A. D. P.

So, as far as I have been able to find, it was a woman who first discerned in the English game a subject fit and fruitful for English literature; and though the scholars may have taken away from a much earlier lady the old honour of writing our first standard treatise on angling, I hardly see them detaching Miss Mitford from her pride of place in the cricket field. I have watched a mother, in the south country to which this authoress belonged, following the exploits of her son, a nice whippy fastish bowler who may yet grow to be a demon among the great, with a delight and a criticism illustrating how even Miss Mitford was after all merely finding words for the spirit of many of similar faith. A passionate soul, she knows no reason why she should not talk all day about this golden world. Here is one of her letters; it is addressed to that thunderous and incessant historical painter Benjamin Robert Haydon, who if he had concerned himself with cricket would have seen it in terms of towering warriors with bats of iron, and balls of fire. (He once saluted the heavenly bodies before daybreak with some outcries about "those half a dozen cricket balls called worlds.") Besides, at the moment he was in some trouble with debts and borrowings of a stature appropriate to his enormous mental strife. But Miss Mitford is writing him a letter: "Pray are you a cricketer? We are very great ones —I mean our parish, of which we, the feminine members, act audience, and 'though we do not play, o'erlook the balls.'" She has just been to a grand match between Hampshire ("with Mr. Budd") and All England, but how cross she is—how disappointed. Those "ugly old men, whiteheaded and baldheaded (for half of Lord's was engaged in the combat, players and gentlemen)", and all so dressed up —silk stockings!—these, "instead of our fine village lads, with their unbuttoned collars, their loose waistcoats, and the large shirt-sleeves which give an air so picturesque and Italian to their glowing, bounding youthfulness." So there these pompous intruders stood, probably all unaware that Miss Mitford existed, "railed in by themselves, silent, solemn, slow—playing for money, making a business of the thing, grave as judges, taciturn as chess players—a sort of dancers without music, instead of the glee, the fun, the shouts, the laughter, the glorious confusion of the summer game." The very weather was affected by their company, and Miss Mitford stood shivering and yawning and moping in her marquee, with "the curse of gentility on all our doings." In spite of all this, indeed all the more because of it, I should like to see a bust of Mary Russell Mitford set up over the press box at Lord's; or possibly a little group of figures would be best, in which she should be pointing an indignant parasol at old (Rev.) Lord Frederick Beauclerk as he leaves the ground shaking his fist at the wicket-keeper who is holding up a stump in high glory. For Lord's itself and its pre-eminence will always depend on the sunny side of cricket—the village touch—the sweetening of the "science" which Miss Mitford quotes so angrily with the love of the sport, and the humour of the unpredicted. And truly he who sees present-day cricket at Lord's on many occasions is almost back to the country green and its felicity.

With Miss Mitford, but second to her in chronological order, the parent of our cricket literature is always considered to be John Nyren, and his case might well surprise a foreign student of our English library. In Sir Paul Harvey's *Oxford Companion to English Literature*, Nyren with his one book for the pocket, and that a book on a mere game, has received an entry as considerable as those of many authors of an ostensibly higher flight and wider range. Moreover, the original editor of Nyren's *Young Cricketer's Tutor* (1833) was the same man who had first observed and equipped and befriended the genius of John Keats—the great-hearted young schoolmaster, Charles Cowden Clarke; and the most recent editors of Nyren were men so profound and discriminating in all literature and art as Charles Whibley and E. V. Lucas. It must seem strange to such of our friends [1] in far countries as read our books if they chance upon the matter; it may make them reflect anew on what was said about Hamlet's being mad and duly coming to England; but we might provide them with a background and a point of view.

For the English mind is creative, and if not creative it is reconstructive; and though you see it starting out to compose a study on an apparently limited and unambitious subject, you may guess that something beyond the first proposal will very often be produced. As Chaucer, when he was moved to say something about a pilgrimage to Canterbury on which the pilgrims clubbed their tales, felt that a prologue would be useful and pleasant, and then described

---

[1] In his *Dictionary of English and American Literature*, published at Tokyo Professor Takeshi Saito has not missed Nyren; but there is not much about England that this devoted admirer has missed.

a number of men and women with unsurpassed fullness of life, making his prologue by itself a complete and inexhaustible masterpiece, so it comes about with many of our writers in their differing spheres and powers. They intend a work that shall serve the purpose of others, or that is the straightforward suggestion which draws them out in the first instance; they will dispense to all who wish for it their seasoned knowledge of something actual on land or water; but they do not stop there. Life has been too good for them to stop there; the particulars of the chosen business are not fully alive until the characters who flourished over and by means of them and the little world that their existences achieved have been summoned into a sort of eternal bioscope. Or else the writer descants on the material groundwork of his theme until he has made of it something beautiful as well as informative; we do not quite trust to the Euclidean treatment of a subject for its full appeal to our hearers.

The ancestral example of this English graciousness of treatment is *The Compleat Angler* by Izaak Walton who supplies, to be exact, "A Discourse of Rivers, Fish-ponds, Fish and Fishing." "I can truly say," wrote a master of this art of angling two centuries and more after the book appeared, "that I learned more about the ways of our British fish and their haunts and habits and how to catch them from Walton and Cotton than from any subsequent writers." And yet the work has been read by many who never tested its practical precepts, because it has something like the air of a picaresque novel; because in it fishing is only the path into a happy and a not impossible region of lively characters and merry meetings and curious amiable disputations and altogether a perfect sunshine holiday for body and mind in a landscape of leafy luxury. "In writing of it I have made myself a recreation of a recreation. . . . And I am the willinger to justify the pleasant part of it, because though it is known I can be serious at seasonable times, yet the whole Discourse is, or rather was, a picture of my own disposition, especially in such days and times as I have laid aside business, and gone a-fishing with honest Nat and R. Roe; but they are gone, and with them most of my pleasant hours, even as a shadow, that passeth away, and returns not."

Something of this constant freshening of the instruction and definition with the breezes and sunbeams and showers of life and remembrance is found in most of the countless books we have on our sports and pastimes, and the farmer's world, and the naturalist's, and the craftsman's. The subject proper will be found explained, with great eagerness, in clear sentence and striking words. Its importance in relation to other subjects may not always be referred to; it is generally assumed that you are a true believer accepting it, and after that,

Act well your part; there all the honour lies.

But from this plain discipline, this laying down of the right ways and the model, the professor will be found reminiscent, recreational, intent on seeing and making you see what a wealth of nature, in man and round him, has been accessible through this separate field. And this is the virtue of John Nyren, though we cannot dream that he knew methodically anything about writing a book, any more than his contemporary John Lawrence who wrote so gloriously about The Horse—a pair of volumes which he who does not ride, may read. Nyren's advice on the several departments of active cricket is succinct and most of it followed sensibly will still carry the pupil a good way towards excellence. But he has not closed his book when he has told us what to do with a bat and ball and what to avoid. As if by accident, he falls into a history of the Hambledon Men in the old graphic manner, that of Fielding, of Smollett, of Cobbett, of Lamb. Individuals arise, their portraits in words demanding to be liked or hated, laughed at or feared, but never ignored. Cricketers? Yes, that's their qualification. And not only that. Of Shakespeare, among several characteristics, Dr. Johnson observed that "History required Romans, but he gives us Men." Nyren, with his sporting worthies, deserves a similar tribute, and to this day we all seek such a characterisation, when all is said and done, of those whose public display has charmed us. Few can reel off the scores and bowling analyses of Dr. W. G. Grace. Many can mangle (as I fear I have done) one or two of the anecdotes which impress his own Johnsonian character upon us. What was it that my beloved A. P. Scott, who spent the sweltering evening hours in Tokyo with me over poems and Wisden, used to think the most revealing story of these? It ran I think on these lines: Dr. Grace had been given Out, Leg Before Wicket. He pointed out that it could not be. The umpire said it could and it was. The Doctor turned from this deplorable man to the square-leg umpire and said, That was Not Out, wasn't it? The poor fellow referred the Almighty back to the bowler's umpire. "Huh," said Dr. Grace, "well, let's get on with the game." They did.

Nyren did not live to see this arch-character of cricket, but he exercised his talent for sharp sketches on some almost equally tough predecessors. He has not a great deal to say of their scores or their bowling analyses (which in any case would be casual matters in his time). He gives us not names and numbers but men, or ghosts—they appeared and walked in the noonday of his youth, more than mortal, yet like mortals. "David Harris . . . was by trade a potter. . . . He was a man of so strict a principle, and such high honour, that I believe his moral character was never impeached. I never heard even a suspicion breathed against his integrity, and I knew him long and intimately. . . . I never busied myself about his mode of faith, or the peculiarity of his creed; that was his own affair, not mine, or any other being's on earth; all I know is, that he was an ' *honest man*,' and the poet has assigned the rank of such a one in creation. It would be difficult, perhaps impossible, to convey in writing an accurate idea of the grand effect of Harris's

bowling; they only who have played against him can fully
appreciate it. His attitude when preparing for his run previously to delivering the ball, would have made a beautiful
study for the sculptor. Phidias would certainly have taken
him for a model." . . . We have seen bowlers who could
in their turn answer to such a description, and some will
name one name above all—for no athlete ever outdid the
grace of E. A. Macdonald.

Portraiture in our country, alike in writing and painting,
has been peculiarly vigorous and eloquent—life in every line.
The conversation piece has been wonderfully well practised,
as Mr. Sacheverell Sitwell has shown in one of his beautiful
volumes of appreciation. The touch of humour has been
there without diminishing the identity and the likeness of
each subject. Nyren, whose professed occasion for figuring
as an author was no more than the popularising of a game,
lived in the age when sketches from life were being made
by artists and authors with traditional mastery and incomparable gusto; he lived in the day of J. T. Smith, who
delineated with arch malice the ludicrous household of old
Nollekens the sculptor, of Thomas Barnes, whose *Parlia-
mentary Portraits* make us half regret that his powers had to
be transferred to the editorial consolidation of *The Times*,
of Charles Lamb who wrote of "the Old Benchers of the
Inner Temple" so that no bombing of their quiet habitation
and his can ever efface them, of young "Boz" who never
even in Pickwick drew comic character more dexterously
and indelibly than in *Mr. Minns and his Cousin* and *The
Tuggses at Ramsgate*. When this was the prevailing rich state
of character-painting among the authors of Britain, it is
not strange that Nyren with his gallery of Hambledon Men
should be effective too; but the man had in himself, apart
from the general taste and skill of the day, some spark of
genius for recalling these personalities out of the shadows.
Like the earliest reviewer of Nyren and several admirers
since, I must depict *him* in his vein of hearty physical
realism by way of his notice of Tom Walker, or a piece of

it: "Tom's hard, ungainly, scrag-of-mutton frame; wilted apple-john face (he always looked twenty years older than he really was); his long, spider legs, as thick at the ancles as at the hips, and perfectly straight all the way down—for the embellishment of a calf in Tom's leg, Dame Nature had considered would be but a wanton superfluity. Tom was the driest and most rigid-limbed chap I ever knew; his skin was like the rind of an old oak, and as sapless. . . . he moved like the rude machinery of a steam-engine in the infancy of construction, and when he ran, every member seemed ready to fly to the four winds. He toiled like a tar on horse-back." We should half expect to see this energumen at last caught and bowled by Mr. Tom Jones, or calling at the back door of the parsonage to ask if Miss Jane Austen would care for a few walnuts.

About this straightforward book, which is not the least ever offered in a land of true humorists to the Comic Spirit, a degree of mystery lingers; we all speak naturally of Nyren, but who actually wrote Nyren's *Cricketer's Tutor*? It has been argued or maintained that Nyren did not. The Baconian Society might go into this matter as soon as they have used up all the literature of the age of Elizabeth. After all, it is no light thing that the authorship of the earliest separate cricket classic should be still undecided, like that of *Baron Munchausen*, *The Letters of Junius* and *The History of John Bull*; but there is no school of thought in the present instance that would travel for a solution beyond two names. The original title-page announces that the *Cricketer's Tutor* is "by John Nyren," and the addendum—the precious part —"by the same author"; yet the lover of the concealed hint may be exercised by what follows, "The whole collected and edited by Charles Cowden Clarke." In what sense "collected"? Moreover in his introduction Clarke quietly refers to "our little chronicle." It may be that the earliest reviewer to whom I have alluded, Leigh Hunt, who was friends with both Nyren and Clarke, has happened to trans-mit the truth of the business by styling the work "Messrs.

Clarke and Nyren's pleasant little relishing book" and by adding, in defence of the third of these epithets, "Relishing this book may be truly called; for Mr. Nyren remembers, and Mr. Clarke records, every thing with a right taste; masculine as the game, and pleasant as the punch after it." In the memoir of Nyren in the *Dictionary of National Biography*, the origin of the book is described without hesitation; Nyren came to the glorious parties at the house of Vincent Novello, and Novello's son-in-law Clarke took the opportunity of jotting down his lusty talks in remembrance of the cricketers of his time. Apparently they could do this in spite of the seas of harmony rolling over them from Novello at the organ.

XI

Back to Malory

WE may think then that Nyren was the author of whom Cowden Clarke was the author, much in the same way as, according to a witty professor of poetry, Wordsworth was Coleridge's greatest poem. However this may be, it looks as though, no Cowden Clarke, no Nyren's Old Cricketers; and when a bust of Nyren is placed alongside that of Miss Mitford in some Poet's Corner to be at Lord's, the chubby and benevolent features of Clarke might be there too in some adjacent presentment. To have awakened the boy John Keats to a sense of all the arts but above all that art in which he added at twenty-three or four a fresh perfection to our plenteous poetry; to have done this, and twenty-five years afterwards to have drawn out the veteran John Nyren and obtained for the public good, in perpetuity, these verbal vitalities of the sunniest game in the world—this is no small double achievement for one man. It is unknown if Clarke's own performances in the field were notable in his day; but a phrase of his from his retreat near Genoa at the age of nearly ninety suggests that he could move between wickets. Describing the attempt of some fellow (during the Regency) to hold him up in a lonely way—Clarke had walked twelve miles to see Mrs. Siddons or Edmund Kean, and was walking twelve miles back—the old man says, "I put on my cricketing speed and ran forward with a swiftness that few at that time could outstrip." Dare I conjecture that this jubilant energy of Clarke outdoors had something to do with the inspiration that he gave to his pupil Keats, whose poetical work glows so superexcellently above almost all others with the physical glory of life? But such players as have not looked at Keats's poems must not blame me if they are now tempted to try it and find that *The Grasshopper and Cricket* does not (except perhaps from the point of view of one fielding on the boundary by the long grass) refer to their favourite game.

How is it that cricket has not called forth more poems of the higher quality? I should have thought George Meredith would have left us at least one of the sort, descriptive, fanciful, analytical a reading of pastime, a necessary supplement to a reading of earth. Why does he tantalise us so, with just a line or two in that picturesque and characteristical ballad *Juggling Jerry*? He has said more in prose, but that will not do for me; Meredith's poems are his final achievement. What a painting in words of some perennial match in the shelter of the Surrey hills he ought to have left us, with what philosophical hints on the spirit of ideal conflict and the resolution of care and strain ! Not so much a dusty answer as no answer at all. In the end, we have a few agreeable songs for cricket by E. V. Lucas and Norman Gale, and a ballade by Andrew Lang—but not much that travels on its own power as poetry into a general anthology. Perhaps only one piece has accomplished that, and it is strange that it sprang from the heart of a mystic, the one who wrote *The Hound of Heaven*. A haunted man, he could not even sit at a cricket match, enjoying it deeply, without seeing phantoms and hearing the voices of the world like muffled bells:

> And I look through my tears at a soundless-clapping host,
>> As the run-stealers flicker to and fro,
>>> To and fro.

But a single poem, we may be sure, is not the total of a man; it is a conception, very possibly, which does not even correspond to his normal being, and nothing more startling could be offered to the cynic who wishes to believe that the poetical man is drifting in a permanent pink cloud than

Francis Thompson's essay on Prince Ranjitsinhji's *Jubilee Book of Cricket*. "In all sobriety"—the words were Mr. J. L. Garvin's—"do we believe him of all poets to be the most celestial in vision, the most august in faculty." In all sobriety, when he examines Ranjitsinhji's precise instructions to cricketers, Francis Thompson writes with as much of the scientific aspect as C. B. Fry, or Hedley Verity, and discourses on the position of the batsman's hands on the bat-handle in forward play and other fine points with the highest seriousness and evident personal contact. But he finds room in his review for a brilliant sketch of Vernon Royle as policeman at cover-point, and he observes—the observation comes enchantingly from the author of *The Hound of Heaven*—"Genius tells in cricket as in all else."

And so the silentish man who sat down next to us and sat in his place all through the lunch intervals without troubling to eat anything was—a visionary whom thousands would have given much to set eyes on, one whose words have become a national possession: and while he sat there, something else was happening to him than the comparison of Kortright's pace with Spofforth's:

> Still with unhurrying chase,
>   And unperturbed pace,
> Deliberate speed, majestic instancy,
>   Came on the following Feet,
>   And a Voice above their beat—
> "Naught shelters thee, who will not shelter Me."

But there are less promising places in which to come upon strange and remarkable men than the cricket crowd.

While I have been waiting for my bookshelves to produce to me, from their veteran ranks, some serene poem on cricket—book-lovers know how shelves if well treated can do such things—a new book arrives and changes the situation. It is in prose and some of it has been appearing, like

Nyren's notices of the cricketers of his time, in a weekly periodical—has been waited and watched for there by old and young. Mr. R. C. Robertson-Glasgow gathers the first volume of his *Cricket Prints* as if to assure us that war is after all an interloper, and peace the regular occupant. He has certain strong advantages. He is a first-class cricketer, and sees everything; can detect why a particular move was made, or anticipate its coming. With that, he is a master of the varieties of personal force and trait; he glories in them, is the natural historian of characters, gathers them as so many fruits from a branch-bended orchard of all kinds. How he commends them with terms of wonder, and whimsicality, and comic suggestion, and moral esteem, indeed with all that his affection can summon to the banquet—like Charles Lamb writing his love-verses to Tobacco.

In this appreciative art, though the author was destined for the cricket-field and its least grass-blade is his, yet I can deplore a little the modifications of time and the limitations of theme. Modern cricketers are, like the mass of us, less picturesquely different from one another than the old; they seem to be set on appearing all alike outwardly, and on concealing any special temperament or distinction within. They are all, from what I have seen and heard of them, charming men; and I know that Mr. Robertson-Glasgow has a beautiful skill in presenting them to our reading one by one in a variety of personal natures. But I could wish that he had been able to catch in the world about him figures of the old sportsman tradition whose characteristics were so untamed and open and robust and ready for the master hand to depict. It should have been R.-G. who went to capture in his gusto and his phrase the Honourable William Hastings, a seventeenth-century centenarian. The portrait as it has come down the ages was not so much the man's own form ("He was very low, very strong, and very active, of a reddish flaxen hair; his clothes green cloth, and never all worth, when new, five pounds") as all that he surrounded himself with; and here are some details:

"His house was perfectly of the old fashion, in the midst of a large park well stocked with deer, and near the house rabbits to serve his kitchen; many fish ponds; great store of wood and timber; a bowling green in it, long, but narrow, and full of high ridges; it being never levelled since it was placed: they used round sand bowls; and it had a banqueting house like a stand, a large one, built in a tree.

"He kept all manner of sport hounds, that ran buck, fox, hare, otter and badger; and hawks, long and short wing'd. He had all sorts of nets for fish; he had a walk in the New Forest; and in the manor of Christ Church: this last supplied him with red deer, sea and river fish. And indeed all his neighbours' grounds and royalties were free to him; who bestowed all his time on these sports, but what he borrowed, to caress his neighbours' wives and daughters; there being not a woman, in all his walks, of the degree of a yeoman's wife, and under the age of 40, but it was extremely her fault, if he was not intimately acquainted with her. This made him very popular; always speaking kindly to the husband, brother, or father, who was to boot very welcome to his house whenever he came.

"There he found beef, pudding, and small beer, in great plenty; a house not so neatly kept as to shame him or his dusty shoes; the great hall strewed with marrow bones, full of hawks' perches, hounds, spaniels, and terriers; the upper side of the hall hung with the fox skins of this and the last years killing; here and there a poll cat intermixed; game-keepers' and hunters' poles in great abundance.

"The parlour was a great room as properly furnished. On a great hearth, paved with brick, lay some terriers, and the choicest hounds and spaniels. Seldom but two of the great chairs had litters of young cats in them, which were not to be disturbed; he having always three or four attending him at dinner, and a little white round stick of fourteen inches long, lying by his trencher, that he might defend such meat as he had no mind to part with to them.

"The windows, which were very large, served for places to lay his arrows, cross-bows, stone-bows, and other such like accoutrements. The corners of the room, full of the best chose hunting and hawking poles. An oyster table at the lower end; which was of constant use, twice a day, all the year round. For he never failed to eat oysters, before dinner and supper, through all seasons; the neighbouring town of Pool supplied him with them.

"The upper part of the room had two small tables, and a desk, on the one side of which was a Church Bible, and, on the other, the Book of Martyrs. On the tables were hawks' hoods, bells, and such like; two or three old green hats, with their crowns thrust in, so as to hold ten or a dozen eggs, which were of a pheasant kind of poultry; which he took much care of, and fed himself. In the hole of the desk were store of tobacco pipes that had been used.

"On one side of this end of the room was the door of a closet, wherein stood the strong beer and the wine, which never came thence but in single glasses, that being the rule of the house exactly observed. For he never exceeded in drink, or permitted it.

"On the other side was the door into an old chapel, not used for devotion. The pulpit, as the safest place, was never wanting of a cold chine of beef, venison pasty, gammon of bacon, or great apple pye, with thick crust extremely baked. His table cost him not much, though it was good to eat at.

"His sports supplied all but beef and mutton; except Fridays, when he had the best of salt fish (as well as other fish) he could get; and was the day his neighbours of best quality most visited him. He never wanted a London pudding, and always sung it in with ' My pert eyes therein-a.' He drank a glass or two of wine at meals; very often syrup of gilly-flowers in his sack; and had always a tun glass without feet stood by him, holding a pint of small beer, which he often stirred with rosemary.

"He was well natured, but soon angry; calling his servants bastards and cuckoldy knaves; in one of which he often spoke truth to his own knowledge, and sometimes in both, though of the same man. He lived to be an hundred; never lost his eyesight, but always wrote and read without spectacles; and got on horseback without help. Until past fourscore, he rode to the death of a stag as well as any."

Cricket crowds being what they are, I do not despair of hearing some day that Mr. Robertson-Glasgow has happened upon the Honourable William Hastings lurking behind the pavilion at Taunton, setting night-lines for weasels or hewing himself a bat from the woodwork; and when this happens the descriptive fragment which I rescue will be filled in with richness. But Mr. Robertson-Glasgow's present art, suited to the age and the subjects accessible to him, is more metaphysical. He has to probe the hidden meanings of his worthies, and hardly will any of them help much by some telling little external hint, such as wearing a revolver holster on a snake-hook belt, or even the display of mutton-chop whiskers. Occasionally even now a mannerism is at his service; it will certainly be well observed, and well intertwined with the general allegorical and interpretative process, almost as if John Bunyan was at the author's elbow. "This sudden griping and grasping of the bat handle doth bewray an inner anguish," etc. Of Philip Mead, one of the many Best Batsmen of All Time who are sure to arise in any sustained cricket talk, Mr. Robertson-Glasgow's active-service memories assemble into this delightful impression: "He was number four. Perhaps two wickets had fallen cheaply; and there the cheapness would end. He emerged from the pavilion with a strong, rolling gait; like a long-shoreman with a purpose. He pervaded a cricket pitch. He occupied it and encamped on it. He erected a tent with a system of infallible pegging, then posted inexorable sentries. He took guard with the air of a guest who, having been offered a week-end by his host, obstinately decides to reside for six months. Having settled his whereabouts with the umpire, he wiggled the toe of his left boot for some fifteen seconds inside the crease, pulled the peak of a cap that seemed all peak, wiggled again, pulled again, then gave a comprehensive stare around him, as if to satisfy himself that no fielder, aware of the task ahead, had brought out a stick of dynamite. Then he leaned forward and looked at you down the pitch, quite still. His bat looked almost laughably broad."

It would never do for me to continue among the choice wits, and the connoisseurs of human nature, who have delighted the public with writings similar to Mr. Robertson-Glasgow's since his favourite Victorian, the Reverend James Pycroft. I should be lying awake o' nights, wondering how ever to come to an end, and trembling at the prospect of being excluded from some great match by a gate-keeper who identified me as the man who had omitted Old Ebor from the pantheon or not said the right thing about Colonel Philip Trevor's prose. Neville Cardus Societies in the northerly parts of the island would be on my track for some loose and humorous allusion to musical analogies, though I hope I should not be deficient in my general devotion to that most eloquent, and not too easily pleased, interpreter of cricket. I might be pardoned by Elton Ede for the vanity of quoting a letter of his, occasioned by a slight attempt to let him know of the pleasure which some of his critical accounts of play had given me. But while the names crowd upon me, from Felix to Fender, from Wisden to Warner, and (on a different track) from Cuthbert Bede to J. C. Masterman, the dream of some virtuous and placid Second Innings in a better world glimmers into view; a blissful time, when under the eye of Cordelia, who reads all books, and supplied by her with a bibliography of cricket books, I shall have a tolerable acquaintance with them all, and never forget or breed erroneous notions of one. In short, if dreams are not all doomed to failure, I may in the end pass for a worthy disciple of that cricket-shelf and all-library bookman, E. V. Lucas.

The other world has surely been appointed in such

manner that E. V. L. has had the fullest talks with his "pocket Shakespeare" Charles Lamb. How they will have exulted together in a thousand twinkling memories of the Town, of the play, the picture galleries, the South Coast, and Paris; and in high and bold debate on the religions, and the principles of poetry, and the essentials of hock and of whisky, and the progress of cookery since that bright hour when roast pig came into human ken. But I guess that E. V. L. will ask Elia at times for something more than the text of Elia itself delivers; and in particular he will scarcely fail to dwell on a little paper written in 1825, called *Readers Against the Grain*. Do you remember it? Lamb is complaining, pretending to complain that the country is going to the dogs. "Young men who thirty years ago would have been play-goers, punch-drinkers, cricketers, etc., with one accord are now—Readers!—a change in some respects, perhaps, salutary, but I liked the old way best." Voices reach me from afar: "Mr. Lamb, if I may still trouble you with questions, were you perhaps one of these same cricketers in your early days?" "My boy—I don't like to boast but I once caught a swallow flying, so you may suppose I was a useful fieldsman.—What a pity we haven't a bat and ball handy. Probably up here they don't go beyond a silly battledore and shuttlecock.—Well, to go on, somewhere about the year ninety-three—1793—I was watching the Gentlemen of Surrey—*your* old friends. . . ."

The reading of cricket literature would scarcely be at an end in a lifetime; and yet it is a mere part of the glorious plethora of writings on sport which have grown up in old England. Indeed, but this also has to be said just now softly, cricket literature is scarcely so rich as that of many other forms of sport—the contemporaries of Charles Lamb did not count it a serious rival to the forceful and jubilant muses of the boxing ring, the racecourse, the hunting field, and to this day the eloquence of those muses is grandly alive. *The Chace*, a poem, penned by squire William Somerville of Warwickshire two centuries ago, stands like a stately fron-

tispiece before an immense assemblage of lusty open-air
prose and verse; and perhaps *The Fancy* by dashing young
J. H. Reynolds, the friend of Keats, holds a similar position
in respect of the boxing literature of England. I have a
theory that, as a gateway some distance away from both
these symbolic classics in their kind, we might find an
earlier and a much plumper work in position. He who wrote
it, in order to lessen the glooms of old age and imprison
ment, was an evident country squire with infinite appetite
for sporting events; "The Noble and Joyous Book Entytled
Le Morte D'Arthur, by Sir Thomas Malory Knyght" is a
register of ferocious and fulminatory Test Matches beyond
my counting played to the finish in a term earlier (we
suppose) than cricket. But Malory stands aside a moment
from the combats and bloodsheddings, to sing the final
praise of a champion, and incidentally to signify that extraordinary wealth of words which has been such a source of
strength to our sporting literature. Hear this old knight
doing justice to another:

"And in every day sir Tristram wold goo ryde on hun-
tynge/for sire Tristram was that tyme called the best chacer
of the world/and the noblest blower of an horne of all
maner of mesures/for as bookes reporte/of syre Tristram
came alle the good termes of venery and of huntynge and all
the syses and mesures of blowynge of an horse/and of hym
we had fyrste all the termes of haukyng/ & which were
beestes of chace and beestes of venery/and which were
vermyns/and all the blastes that longen to all maner of
gamen/Fyrste to the vncoupelynge/to the sekynge/to the
rechate/to the flyghte/to the dethe/and to strake/and many
other blastes and termes/that all maner of gentylmen haue
cause to the worldes ende to preyse sir Tristram and to
praye for his soule."

XII

Incorrigibles

HARDLY had I copied this fragment, so unlike the usual tributes paid by Malory to his death-dealing knights, and so indicatory of the rich resource of our language in terms for all the details of our sports and games, when an old volume standing next to that on King Arthur appealed to me in the way these old volumes have. "Will you not disturb the dust on me, flatter me ever so little by being a reader for a moment?" It was a capacious collection of *Statutes at Large*, and in a little while I chanced upon the Englishman whom we know, though *anno* XVII. *Edwardi Quarti* he was as yet no great cricketer. But his ball-game tendencies alarmed some of the authorities, and morality was ready with laws to reform him. "Item," they said, "whereas by the lawes of this Land no person should use any unlawful games, as Dice, Coites, Tenis, and such like games, but that every person strong and able of bodie should use his bow, because that the defence of this land was much by Archers, contrary to which Lawes the games aforesaid and many new imagined games, called Closh, Kailes, Halfe-bowle, Handin and Handout, and Quekeborde be daily used in divers partes of this land, as well by persons of good reputation as of small behaviour: And such evil disposed persons that doubt not to offend God in not observing their holy dayes, nor in breaking the lawes of the lande to their own impoverishment, and by their ungracious procurement and incouraging, doe bring other to such games, till they be utterly undone and impoverished of their goods." . . . In short, any one who should play Closh, Kailes and the rest would get two years in prison and pay a fine of £10, a sum of money which closh-players do not have.

What came of this enactment? I can only suppose that the Closh Clubs went on cheerfully closhing, for my old volume opened at a later page headed *Anno* XXXIII. *Henrici Octavi*. At first I imagined my attention was being directed, like that of Henry VIII. himself, to persons who practised invocations and conjurations of spirits, by way of discovering buried treasure or destroying their neighbours; but the next Act was the one which it was meant I should observe. "An Act for the maintenance of Artillerie, debarring unlawfull games." The historians who happen to read this page will forgive me for referring to a not wholly forgotten statute, which was brought about, it appears, by the Bowiers, Fletchers, Stringers and Arrowhead-makers of this realm. They had been getting short of employment, and all because of those games-players, who "had found, and daily find, many and sundrie new and craftie games and plaies, as logating in the fields, slide thrift, otherwise called shove-groat" . . . Hamlet as we have all noticed had some notion of logats. But he would have found himself by this law constrained to give up his Bowling, Coiting, Tennis and any lately invented games, and put himself to the long bow; that is, if he went about among his poorer subjects. The law had been discreetly framed. Noblemen who could find space for Bowls or Tennis within the precincts of their houses had nothing to pay, and it may be that they might even captain teams at Closh or Cloish without the chilling apparition of a constable.

Among the personages who have always had my admiration, the policemen who stand during the matches by the bowling-screen at Lord's are now in my memory. Far away in time though they are, the ancient statutes hover about them, and one has a faint sense of guilt; yet they appear to look on the game with forgiveness, and will even return the ball after some indignant blow by Edrich with a grandeur blended with dexterity. It is rather as though William Wordsworth had decided to contemplate the game and relate it to life's deeper issues, allowing it some decasyllabic verses, which do not appear among his ascertained MSS.:

> Nor, by the tenor of the sport unpleased,
> Shall I withhold my tribute to this game
> Perchance from deeper wisdom than appears
> Developed, as, if truth tradition speak,
> That other game scarce speedier of result,
> Chess, was by some old general devised
> To keep his army from a mutiny.

In early years, I was always a little bewildered by the annual appearance of a team on our ground, entitled the Constabulary. They were not (to the material eye) in uniform, but without its aid they had a manner which, as I gather from Captain Osbert Sitwell's reminiscences, would have caused the late W. H. Davies, for all his wish to stand and stare, thoughtfully to make a wide circuit.

What the proper explanation is that a modern Wordsworthian should give for his presence to a constable on his night beat I hardly know. Again, through the darkness, an ancient statute hovers about the form of the constable; he has still some inherited inclination to apprehend all vagrom men, night-walkers—and what is a man who stands and stares at midnight? I was loitering in an enchanted, embalmed darkness a few summers ago on a little bridge, where I had haunted as a child; the unseen stream was talking, a whole lifetime was talking—but suddenly my circumstances were being dryly investigated by a careful policeman who did not easily follow my train of thought. But then Wordsworth himself was in favour of moving the gypsies on, alleging that their life was " torpid." They still camp in the lost places, but Scholar Gypsies are not for this age.

"Why . . .?" "Because . . ." I am afraid that modern life has been falling into this trap. "Come, come, you must know. Just tell the Court what you had in mind when . . ."

Yes, sometimes the answer is there, or is fortunately impro-
vised, and the machine gives a peremptory yet satisfied click.
But we are becoming the nervous slaves of a formula. The
blanks have to be filled up with rapid definites. They may
not seem to refer to *our* chances at all—going our rounds,
we have not noticed these sub-divisions, these clauses, these
one-word descriptions—but unless we promptly do something about it and get our lives into these pigeon-holes *on
nous aura*. The case is all the stranger since we have heard
so much this century of the increase in psychological science,
and the realisation of the complexity of our life; and here
we are, badgering one another for the return of the crude
form by 8 a.m. on the 15th inst. with the particulars filled
in, in block letters, but (if not in the Z2 category) see foot-
note J. Why did you not, or why did you? Are you, or are
you not? Would you, or wouldn't you?

For this reason (but I am in peril of exemplifying the
process which I have ventured to regret) let us extol and
let us delight in the Cricket Field and the visionary and
"unimportant" game and prowess which belong to it.
There at least (it will soon come again) you may have even
at its headquarters a Rover's Ticket, and you may always
stray securely aloof from the austerities lined up in the
world outside the turnstiles. There you are at liberty and
need not talk about it, neither will any one start in upon
you with demands that you should study it in detail and
make out a table of its superior qualities. The occasion in
most parts of the world is sunshine, and the time is youth
—for these seniors round you when they slipped away from
their offices dropped their burden of age, and the boys and
girls are all excitement and dream. The ceremony we witness
is graceful, and unless some unfortunate batsman plays a
ball with his ear or his ribs it exacts no sacrifice; it requires
moreover no thesis on our part, no lopping and planing of
the mind's branchings and twigs so as to produce a blunt
"opinion," or article of belief. There will be triumphs of
individuals and triumphs of bodies corporate—and there

will be none. If a cat chooses to take a walk out into the arena, it will be an incident as memorable as the marvellous technical luxuries we are given; and if one of the boys squeezing under the ropes has the luck to have the ball bounce into his hands and throw it in to the great man in flannels who just failed to overhaul it—the boy knows who he is, as much as he knows who rules Russia—we share his thrill. The next free day we get, perhaps we shall dig the allotment, or saunter in a flower-garden, or climb with the cloud-shadows or float on the river with the moorhens; but this day we give to society without society's strain and struggle. The faces about us are easy. There are good notes in the voices, as when some fine old farmer recognises a thisty companion of the bat and pads after an interval of many years; and I really believe British beer is seldom better than as they are taking it now just in the shade of the marquee, waiting for the appearance, if the cricket gods will, of some one else who has been long absent from their daily tracks. And here they can converse of matters that rise fairly over the red-lit tumults and nightmares of the world since last they met: "Now *she* married young Tim Kettle the piano-tuner," "That never was a house to live in," "They tell me there's a proposal to open up that old channel between Sammons's and the Bellmouth Bend," "The offertory has been slightly better lately." If only the clock would not insist on behaving much like clocks elsewhere, here would be eternity, and the cluster of oaks at the corner of the ground would be a green temple for ever at the entry to so unworldly a place.

But then, the heroes themselves! No men ever wear their laurels more simply. They have more than skill; they have the spirit of the game, of the mystery, and I have watched them often with a yearning that their composure might extend to the contentious world beyond their greensward. We hear occasionally of a strife between even them, and we are glad when the mutterings die away, for it is so little like the prevailing serenity with which they pursue their art. In success, in unsuccess they are equable, and humorous, and sympathetic. This courtesy of theirs, if one could put it into words, might convert the most obstinate enemies of cricket; and I have never ceased to feel a little unsatisfied when, off the field, the press tells me something of one or other of them which stamps them as frail mortals after all. But that is "off the field," outside the charmed circle, outside their especial destiny; and on other days or hours than those when the complete secret of cricket unites them and us in a very perfect gentle island of innocence.

"Many a green isle needs must be" in the map of humanity, and many another way to it than that which the steps of Englishmen have worn to their cricket grounds, which nevertheless are their nearest form of dream country. There are judges of the character of Englishmen who say that they are satisfied with a fact, and only with that. I fear that they are concealing something from their critics, who however need go no farther than, in London, St. John's Wood or Kennington to correct their short view, and discover the poetic truth. The Englishman is reluctant to discover it in himself, and perhaps would never go much further in a general theory of the immortal tradition of Lord's than what is contained in these lines by an old, prosaic poet:

> 'Tis morning: well; I fain would yet sleep on;
>   You cannot now; you must be gone
>   To court, or to the noisy hall;
> Besides, the rooms without are crowded all;
>   The stream of business does begin,
> And a spring-tide of clients is come in.
> Ah, cruel guards, which this poor prisoner keep!
>   Will they not suffer him to sleep?
> Make an escape; out at the postern flee,
> And get some blessed hours of liberty:
> With a few friends, and a few dishes dine,
>   And much of mirth and moderate wine.

To thy bent mind some relaxation give,
And steal one day out of thy life, to live. . . .

Moreover, Grace is batting; or Jessop; or McCabe; or your favourite batsman—but I should have thought you would be satisfied with those.

XIII

Paint me Cricket

AND yet, how many of us, when there is no war, make haste across the Channel at the season when these champions and the game which bred them are at their best. I am one of these vagabond Englishmen. My reasons? It is possible to name "of many, one": I enjoy the picture galleries abroad; and this I believe will scarcely be regarded by any one as a lamentable excuse. There is no substitute for the Louvre, I take it, or the collections at Munich, or Antwerp, or Brussels; and if it be asserted that the world's masterpieces can all be seen in reproductions, I need not go into that question but maintain apart from it that I can only see multitudes of remarkable lesser paintings by travelling to them. "Remarkable" has two directions. I have a private delight, which I. R. and I think we understand as well as most, in hunting for the sublimely ridiculous in continental art, which yields us quite a menagerie under the class name of Wappers. Baron Wappers, of Antwerp and Belgium, is gone, but his name will live outside Belgium if we have any future opportunities of research. Rubens himself has provided us with magnificent specimens of the Wappers way.

Still, in these years of non-Channelling, this zest for pictures has not been forced to wither; and an early and restless suspicion that our own British School has been neglected or undervalued by our instructors has grown within me, and "ripened into certainty." Evidences greet me at every turn. At Nottingham the other day (and it was my first visit to the city since the Australian cricketers drew me among the host to Trent Bridge) two small oil paintings in a window pulled me up; and you, Cordelia, were caught as well. Not that they had anything dramatic or extraordinary in them. One was a scene of half a dozen windmills, the other a landscape with rising ground; and they were painted about a century ago, by H. Smyth. He or she has not a mention even in that too little known but glorious work, *The Old English Landscape Painters*, wherein Colonel M. H. Grant displayed several hundreds of them who have not had the appreciation due. H. Smyth's windmills, if it was not something in the moment and the mood which made us think this, were painted as true companions of the wind and sky, so lightly they rose from their knoll, so glitteringly they towered. I do not doubt their ability to work; they were not part of a *ferme ornée*. But there was a free joy, a clear spirit about them, such as made us feel that H. Smyth of whom I know no more was happy in a delicate apprehension and the means of expressing it.

And that province of country scenes is one in which our painters, "so many and so many" (so that we know them geographically as Smith of Chichester, Archer of Derby, Barker of Bath, Turner of Oxford and all those hearts who followed Crome of Norwich) have never gone wrong. They have possibly excelled our poets and our Selbornian authors in their infinite capacity and religion for watching Nature and translating her beauties and her felicities. They have taken delight in the figures of the men and women and children who have not lost the primeval relation with this goddess and mother, and their sympathetic eye has chosen well among the toils, the implements, the doings and diversions of the year "ten miles from town," or a hundred. Nor is this English aptitude in one kind of painting in the least danger of dying out. In London this year, a London as yet showing pitiful gaps and sad fragments and vast wounds caused by the bitterest war, there have been exhibited the most delightful topographical water-colours by many hands, equal with all but the greatest of long ago—but Girtin and Cotman and De Wint, even Farington and Daniell may baffle all the host for a long age.

De Wint, whose "rich surprise" seems inexhaustible, and who paints always on a grand scale even when he passes his day with minor topics, is among those who have painted a cricket match; he has not taken liberties (as some artists did) with the game, which looks a perfectly good one in his picture; but he treats it as an incident animating the landscape, to which it is as congenial and contributory as any group of country people or of cattle or horses and goats and sheep. In this sense it is a blessing to have so profoundly truthful an artist as De Wint on my side, for my mind constantly turns to this naturalness of the cricket field and its inhabitants at their gentle occupation. There is a time in life when the game itself in the progress of its dramas and attainments and all that can be done by its devotees must appear as a sufficient thing, insulated from the rest of the affairs and colours of life. I am well past that time, and yet I can be more deeply and sweetly moved by cricket now than when the scores, styles, surprises, triumphs, new methods were all distinct to me; when I could not dream that I should ever be so degraded as to forget a name or an initial of any who figured in county teams, or which team stood third or forth in the championship in such and such a season. Alas, I have forgotten those and other former treasures of learning collected so easily and exultantly in boyhood. Where now are those proudly penned specifications of the most magnificent church organs in the world? I am barely capable now of noting the number of the keyboards, and the existence of couplers, or pedals. But, in this matter of cricket and De Wint, I like to believe that time has more than compensated for the slackening of my concern with the particulars. I see no longer a series of talents recording themselves, with fortune often playing some trick on her wheel on them, in results and in distinctions. They are playing there with their wonted singleness of purpose in the summer light, but the forms merge into my picture of nature, never to be painted, so soon does it flow into the inner and incommunicable spirit. The dream is one in which these happy preoccupied folk are no longer cricketers, nor the old man with the scythe on the lane side any longer a labourer; but all, with the trees and streams and hills and hazy distances and pavilion clouds, are a finely wrought mantle worn by—a mystery. Nature is not yet less than that.

Something like that reverie, however finer and fuller it was, governed the paintings of Peter De Wint, which have a composure like that of great odes, and which beautifully gather all circumstance into a complete and instantly impressive feeling. But as a painter he might comment that he was conscious only of representing with the materials at his disposal a receding countryside which his eye was trained to see in full proportions. In the book by Colonel Grant of which I spoke—a book that belongs to the rank of those in which England is mirrored in her fertile and inimitable excellence—there are two or three paintings of cricket by other men. One of them is Francis Hayman, an eighteenth century painter who had his idolaters; and his *Cricket Match*, usually seen in the gallery of the Marylebone Club in the pavilion at Lord's, is accurate in respect of the game. Yet, like De Wint, he paints this stern contest on the Royal Artillery Ground as a kind of fête champetre within and integral with a landscape, and the spectator thinks of the whole delightful scene and mood of the season rather than the array and proceedings on the shaven green. I find it so in another picture, by mild unapplauded Read of Bedford; it comes to us with plenty of cricket, and it belongs to the greater glory, summer days and bounteous beauty, the world like a coloured butterfly resting warm on a sunny stone.

It does not matter much if this reflectiveness on cricket and what lies beyond and above it comes over me at a moment when I am taking part in a game; this has been happening, and must lead to my retiring by common consent, apart from other implacable causes, from the ranks of playing members. At Nuneham Courtenay this very sum-

mer, when I was presumed to be keeping wicket, the game
itself grew dim, the action lost its precision and importance,
and only that sweet-breathing, singing, shining, swaying,
rejoicing universe of nature about us had any existence for
me. To be sure, the pleasant company of the young
cricketers, their physical fineness and their high spirits were
all concerned in that magic tale; but it was sheer luck that
some horrid error of mine did not ruin all in my distant
contemplations. Often have I fancied with alarm that a
reverie like mine might fall upon some player in the upper
house of cricket where errors matter, and in a Test Match
itself distract him gently but irresistibly from his function:
but heaven will avert this. And it is an argument in favour
of such austere cricket grounds, untinged with mysticism,
unless the ghost of Francis Thompson radiates a faint
luminous haze, as Old Trafford.

Paintings of cricket and cricketers must in the main
belong to that immense though still unmeasured range of
pictures called into being by British sport, and cannot compare for number or for energy of creation with those of the
hunting field and the horse race. No George Stubbs, no
Ben Marshall ever came to find such occasions and subjects
in the cricket field as these which were so much enjoyed by
the gentlemen of England, King Lear included. The game,
after all, has no such costume and paraphernalia as the field
sports, and the animal creation since the decline of the old
horses who got promptly into the shafts of the roller when
No. 11 went in to bat has been missing from it. I can hardly
see a patron of cricket even in the lordliest period having
his picture done as he led in his favourite umpire among
the cheering onlookers. The thought of the sporting artists
(one day their modern countrymen will awake to their
genius) sends me back to some evenings which I can never
hope to enjoy again, when sometimes at the conclusion of
a cricket match in his village a gentleman of the eighteenth
century stamp would invite me to his table. He had inherited and eagerly extended a large collection of art, but

it was the glory with which he directed my notice to the sporting section of it which enchanted me. His vast rooms were not lit up with any modern brilliance, but his serious enthusiasm created in me the feeling of some illuminate shrine, with an altar-piece (of Newmarket Heath) by Tillemans, and sundry niches sacred to Surtees and Leech. At the time I was too young to consider that such men and such habitations were disappearing from the social system, but the magnificence of the Tillemans and the true though scarcely divine worship which my host had in his soul did not escape me. The oddest thing was (and I suspect his butler would have agreed with me) that this stately old gentleman with his world of the turf and the hunt should have ever given an evening's time, and all else that he so hospitably gave, to a nomadic young poet who came without the slightest proficiency in any field sport. I had fired some shots in my time, but nearly all at German parapets, tree stumps or humps of sandbags which flame-startled darkness transformed into moving enemies. My host had no wish to hear of that use of the gun.

But so King Lear entertained a solitary who managed to find his way into the hall; and I have discovered that by judicious listening a man may even live among consummate cricketers without forfeiting their esteem.

> Where be they before us weren,
> Houndes ledden and hawkes beren,
> And hadden field and wood?

This ancient English lyric was not among the occasional quotations with which I tried to say as little as possible in those vintage conversations at Mulberry Hall.

I have heard the old lord of Mulberry Hall, warmed with the contrast between the cold black tempest outside and the increasing blaze of his own broad hearth, tell a tale or two of a sportive rather than sporting nature. His daughter heard him too, with a little trepidation; but if she feared that he would leave any impression on me through these merry sallies other than that of a true grandee she had no need. He retained, despite his allusions to Port Said in the colourful days (it boasted a few bottles of beer and a devastating brawl of gramophones when I was there), a high seriousness. In fact as I put things together in my mind it was clear that I had previously met him in the society of English characters with whom Shakespeare dined.

"Master Page, I am glad to see you: much good do it your good heart! I wished your venison better; it was ill killed. How doth good Mistress Page?—and I thank you always with my heart, la, with my heart."

"Sir, I thank you."

"Sir, I thank you; by yea and no, I do."

"I am glad to see you, good Master Slender."

"How does your fallow greyhound, sir? I heard say he was outrun on Cotsall."

"It could not be judged, sir."

"You'll not confess, you'll not confess."

"That he will not. 'Tis your fault, 'tis your fault; 'tis a good dog."

"A cur, sir."

"Sir, he's a good dog, and a fair dog: can there be more said? he is good and fair."

There is no need to give these sentences to the several speakers in remembering my old friend, for they all belong to him. "Though we are judges and doctors and churchmen, Master Page, we have some salt of our youth in us; we are the sons of women, Master Page." . . . "And is old Double dead?" "We have heard the chimes at midnight, Master Shallow." "That we have, that we have, that we have."

Looking for the record of my friend in painting, I can scarcely catch him among our home men. I get nearer in the Netherlands, and have almost settled the matter for ever in that grand piece by Teniers of a Château and its seigneur; there he is in his prime, and is receiving a prodigious pike from a stubby old ruffian with a lifetime's official or other network behind him. *He* has seen larger pike, and in brighter condition; "but let it pass—let it pass—we sometimes take a pike for the amusement of the ladies; now J. F. Herring (a suitable name, I think, my friend? ha), now Herring *could* paint angling subjects, and I shall show you the finest fish painting that J. F. Herring ever accomplished. I picked it up for a song at the Plowden sale—you remember poor Whiffler Plowden—O no, you wouldn't—a very compleat angler, but no taste in pictures. Not, that is, unless someone advised him, and my poor father used to advise him a great deal."

Not many miles from Mulberry Hall there lived a local celebrity for whom memory speaks with equal pleasure and elegy with equal sense of loss. He was a farmer, and with brief intervals in most of which I seemed never to encounter him, but I have no doubt they all happened, he lived on horseback. The intervals included games of cricket, and it was from this part of his activities that his name was first sounded to me. I think he was not less known with his gun, or rod, or his flowers and lawns; but in the cricket world of that village country his name was mighty. It was therefore with some fear that our little team heard one July he was playing against us. The match began late, and when we went in the light was going; and he was bowling. The words meant something. There was nothing for it but to guess and slam, and some did not and rued it; so I did, without much delay, and the ball flew into an oak tree somewhere. Jack who was at the other end followed this fortunate example a moment or so later. We carried on till the play had to stop; and then the famous bowler came to us and spread an arm round each and spoke words which we were enchanted to hear. "You boys have eyes like hawks," he said. But I have my suspicions still; he was only half bowling that evening, and those violent smacks into the dusk were as much his work as ours. Beautiful work. He wanted us to go home happy, and after a few pints which he caused to appear without any apparent effort we went in that sense. But I never saw him again; and I can only hope that young cricketers everywhere may some day meet as benevolent an old one.

What I have been recalling from a lost sunburnt pasture beyond the whispering wheatfields and the old bullock-track is a reason why cricket can never be painted in its true light. Its outer forms indeed are a good subject for a part of the painter's conception of an English or perhaps Fijian scene. Charles Dickens opening a match at Gads Hill with a lob, none the less alarming in the anticipation because of his beard, has been recorded in a capital canvas. But that spirit of the game which was so kindly working in our redoubtable farmer-bowler that evening would not appear in any picture that Crome himself could have achieved. Our friend, however, would have enjoyed such a picture, wherein the pastime's little squadrons were as any other figures present, the tribes of evening, gilded with the parting sunbeam. In men like him I have felt that all Nature as they have known her within their hereditary horizons is present; they are the world which they contemplate. Whatever comes therein, whatever the seasons bring forth, whatever the ways of the human brain and heart may there devise and perform, they accept in the circuit of a great providence.

And so, when the years have gradually wrought upon their lives as upon all else, they are masterly in their farewells to what they were. For them there is no repining, though there must ever be the hint of sadness in a resignation.

> We drop like the leaves of the tree
>> And we go,
>> Even we,
>> Even so.

The triumph of life dies away, and the triumph of life opens more widely and profoundly than ever. Our earliest masterpoet has given his most triumphant character (who had surely enjoyed the individual experience as much as any one, and whose story is a riot of colour) the final word,

I have had my world as in my time.

But when does the signal come to us, to bid farewell to the things we had so long supposed of endless age? How strangely it strikes in reading a biography when the subject is described "for the last time taking his favourite walk to the old Encampment," or "playing with his usual gaiety on the piano, thenceforth for ever closed for him"—simple matters, yet subtle in their suggestion of the predestined. We may thank Thomas Hardy for poems on these endings, on the transformation of that which was once so familiar into the unfamiliar, and that which was so near and easy into the unachievable and the inaccessible. "Next year— sometime—never." The shadow on the dial knows as much as we.

For me, imperfectly grown in the contrasts of life, a shade of grief has been falling over this old country game and symbol called cricket, and I can almost feel that Burton should have played his fancy and despair upon it in the *Anatomy of Melancholy*. Even he could scarcely have looked more pensive than some old professional bowlers I have encountered, in whose faces, in whose very boots I could only read the news that mankind invariably plays the wrong stroke to the perfect ball and gets four runs for it—an unspoken Hardyan complaint against high heaven. I do not suffer from that sort of dejection, especially as I do not get the four runs (in eternal series) which apparently cause them to indulge a sadness of soul. No: but from the serious long rhythm of the game in the brightest days, and its measured, numbered, deliberate moving onward and carrying onward into night all its free and merry masters, the ghostly old wizard Time sends me some more poignant message than from many happy things that race by with airy speed and flash of brilliant brevity. It may not be so unusual, this inner voice from the wickets; it may all be part of the English nature; and though the millions who play are most of their time in great spirits, and feel nothing worse than the calamities of missing catches or "failing to trouble the scorers," yet I hear this voice through all.

Then, sometimes, it may be forgiven me if I am unfaithful to the English painters and the English game, and am lured across the Channel, where diversion in life and in art is not so haunted with a trial of endurance and a shade of grief. For a little while after the passage it may happen that the great events at Lord's or Old Trafford, which had only begun to unfold themselves when I was setting forth, disturb my mind; and then, somebody will perhaps fasten on me who is eager to be kind, and thinks that I should be happier in my exile if I knew the latest score. This was the case in Poperinghe a few years since, when a young Englishman of the cleric fashion, resident there, endeavoured to make me at home. He understood by all ordinary usage that a Test Match was one of the things I was in Flanders to discuss; we went into the matter, but my attention wandered. In the end I inquired about the local sports and pastimes, and whether the old archery club had come to life again and fixed up its tall mark and small summerhouse at the Ypres end of the town; this did not appear to him to be a proper subject. He did, however, explain that the inhabitants had some peculiar and out-of-date ways, and that the sanitation was bad. And as he left me, with final instructions for my correct choice of sights and subjects in that un-English country (but we do our best), the Test Match mysteriously left me too. I heard of it again many days afterwards, as though rediscovering some faded photograph and after a restless moment remembering whose it was.

XIV

Rival Sports

"AND are you trying to tell me," asked Cordelia, over-hearing my meditations on my creaky broomstick, "that you would prefer to spend your summer days in some town-end on the continent, waiting for a few archery-lovers to come and shoot clay pipes off a kind of flagstaff? Is this what you secretly long for when you pretend to be watching cricket?" I suppose the answer is no; and the young and moderately muscular Christian at Poperinghe may not have been wrong in thinking the Poperinghe spectacle all very dull. As for the archery, I believe that Ostend would have been the place, when the amateurs of the whole region assembled for contests as great in their way as our own great games—may their next rally be near! But the pursuit of the cherub Recreation, that smiling idle busy one, might lead us well away from the greatest game in the world, so captained and so strategical; and over the way there a simplicity of manners and of living well is to be found, and pastime without tears. It takes hold of me from the first moments of placidity, in the morning sunlight outside the first café.

What (now that we have found our hotel) shall we play at? I am all for Le Jardin Public. But that is not a game. Indeed I think it is, let us say at Saint Omer—for as yet we have not hurried our journey, conceiving that France is France once we are past the douane, if not before. And what is it that makes Le Jardin Public such a pastime here, whereas in England you did not seem to be much exhilarated even by the serpentine paths and spaced trees of the Arboretum? For the answer I must ask you to listen to the Abbé Augustin Dusautoir, in his ideal Tourist's Guide to Saint Omer, since

I am sure that he reveals the spirit of this game at its best, and he that learns from the Abbé will not lack happy hours. It is a question of attitude—

> And Hope is but a fancy-play,
> And Joy the art of true believing.

Come then, "pénétrons maintenant dans le Jardin Public," entering through its monumental iron gate, of finest beauty. The Garden is of vast extent, and picturesque as vast; perfectly planted, constantly tended and kept flowering. Here one breathes an air that is pure, and frequently renewed, of which all classes of society take advantage, especially in the afternoons. But do not miss the main Avenue, the postern constructed by the celebrated Vauban, the monument to M. Martel the benevolent, with its two bronze plaques—which symbolise. . . . Then the parterres, the bosquets! And the artificial lake, and the swans, and the ducks, and the cascade—what a harmony, rocks and verdure forming the most magical coup d'œil.

But there is the little bridge, and the rural hut, and the winding path—remark the variety of the lesser trees among the elms adorning the old earthworks; all sorts and tints of foliage and the whole set in greenness, completing a perspective which is to the last degree restful to the sight. And as for the ear, that organ has for its enchantment a multitude of birds of varied plumage whose inexhaustible twittering joins its joyous note to the concert formed by all the elements of Nature in the *Eden audomarois*. Nor is this all. We still have to visit the botanic garden, the panorama, and perhaps noblest of all, the Kiosk erected in 1896, where on Sundays the Band of the 8th line regiment and the Municipal Band execute their impeccable and attractive concerts.

Such in brief is the Abbé's invitation, and I do not think he is far wrong, either for that Jardin at Saint Omer or for others in similar cities. Perhaps you would not subscribe to the impression which he gives, at the first glance, the first day—it might be pouring rain even in that Eden, and the mute bandstand itself might look miserable. But allow a day or two to have planted you in the country, let the thoughts of the correspondence already piling up at home and of mighty matters from Goodwood to Westminster and Bradford and Liverpool go their ways, and you will find yourself playing a respectable innings already in the game of Le Jardin Public. When you have achieved the height of taking a walk there in the rain on a November day, you may be sure that you have caught for yourself one of the cherubim—even if he looks like an importunate (but municipal) duck at the foot of the unofficial cascade from your hat.

If this leisurely and quiet game, which has many devotees, belongs to the field of daydreams and paradises and some beyond Coleridgean sphere where the body rather floats along than exercises its joints—if its victory in happiness is so delicate a flower that it makes an Abbé talk of enchantments and of spells without a qualm—I have come upon sport more robust and physical in such honest towns as Saint Omer. There was nothing extraordinary in them as shows—some great boys hustling one another around on stilts (not perhaps aware of the mighty stilt-battles which once entertained great personages at Namur), or a set of stubby hoarse gentlemen popping away with toy guns at clay pigeons conveniently suspended in the back streets. Yet in these friendlies it is not impossible to trace a peasant freedom of an ancient make. The players are merry, the day is their own. They make me think of the cheerful little groups of holiday folk in Breughel's paintings, or that one with a ball in the *Colloquies* of Erasmus of Rotterdam, whose talk comes freshly down the centuries, and has a meaning in it for this and for the centuries to come. May I attempt it out of the Latin, for it was not in Latin after all that the sturdy skittle-players of Saint Omer were talking; and Erasmus has written down something like their talk?

Adolph [another Adolph], *Bernard, the Umpires.*

Be. : What's the prize for the winner, or what's the loser to pay?

A .: How about the loser having his ear cut off?

Be. : Or something else a bit more intimate. I don't think much anyway of playing for money. You're a Frenchman, I'm a German; we'll go at it for the honour of our two countries.

Ad. : If I win, you have to shout out three times, Long Live France; if I'm beaten (and God save me from it) I'll do the shouting for Germany.

Be. : I'll take that. I hope my luck's in; and as these two great countries are going to risk themselves in a game, let's have the balls exactly alike.

Ad. : You see that big stone standing a bit away from the gate?

Be. : I've got it.

Ad. : That's the target, and here's the line we throw from. . . .

(And so they throw, and presently) :

Umpires : Germany wins! and what a win, with a loser of this quality.

Be. : Sing up, France.

Ad. : I'm hoarse.

Be. : Why, that's nothing new in a Frenchman; come on man, sing like a cuckoo.

Ad. : Long live Germany three times.

Be. : Here, that's what you were supposed to *sing* three times. . . . Now we've worked up just a tiny thirst; let's get along to the snuggery; and you can finish off your singing there.

Ad. : It's all right by me, if it is by the umpires.

Be. : It's the only thing to do. The Gallic cock will sing a lot better after a little throat lotion.

A Kermesse—defined as "a fair held on the feast day of the patron saint of a church in Holland, Flanders, &c."—is the full utterance of this jollity and native humour, and has produced one of the inextinguishable pleasures of the art of the Low Countries. To us who wander from other traditions into the midst of such occasions, it seems as if the whole city and the countryside for miles were moved by a single impulse of play, and din, and fun: it seems as though the highest manifestations of the day, the bright and sumptuous processions and observances, were of a piece with the random nonsense and the eating and drinking all round. Dull Care needs no warning to be gone; he went yesterday; and now the gladness and mirth which usually have to hide from the sight of those strenuous and capable workers are right in the picture. The strength of their release was brought home to me in a pair of words at Ypres one morning; having arrived in that rebuilt city only the night before, I was not in touch with local affairs, and I stepped out of the hotel by the Ramparts in the sunshine thinking of things in the shadow. Suddenly two young broad-backed broad-faced men out of some smithy in a Jan Steen, and a young woman with a rosy face and that glorious rich plainness of the belles of such pictures, blocked the way and seized me together and demanded a contribution. I got it from my pocket, but I asked for what it was to be given. An amazing, an inexplicable question. "Pour notre fête," answered the blacksmiths and the girl, intense, powerful. All the fame and glory and freedom of the day rang in those voices, and those few words. All Flanders was on the move, not to a war, not to a rebellion—save that of primitive play.

If there is a spiritual home of the steam-organ, surely it is to be found between Arras and Lille and Brussels. In that world, the paintwork, brasswork and blastwork of that extraordinary machine are not too exuberant for the public joy. I almost think that Hazebrouck must have been the spot where one morning, in the middle of the huge *place*, the first, the original example was seen and heard in its new and congenial violence; a creation, prepared perhaps with as much secret industry as that terrifying handkerchief given by "an Egyptian" to the mother of Othello.

> A kobold that had numbered in the forge
> The sun to course two myriad compasses
> In his prophetic fury built the work.

And then—"dansons la gigue," the more the merrier, and tire the sun with holiday. Why, Verlaine is taking a holiday from that school in Lincolnshire.

Over the Flanders which I was beginning to know a huge war had passed, and the roundabouts and the pageants, the reunions and the carillons were all part of the rejoicings over its being a thing of yesterday. I was reminded of *Othello*, and that course of national events which made his personal tragedy so unspeakably bitter.

> "News, friends, our wars are done: the Turks are
> drown'd."

Why, then, on news like that:

> "It is Othello's pleasure, our noble and valiant general, that, upon certain tidings now arrived, importing the mere perdition of the Turkish fleet, every man put himself into triumph; some to dance, some to make bonfires, each man to what sport and revels his addiction leads him."

The name, "The Long Week-End," has been devised to characterise the period between the two great wars, and it has merit; but it does not equal the strength and hope of the long kermesse which was enjoyed in Flanders, and much further afield, during those years of revival and reaffirmation.

What a holiday the world must take when, once again,

it can say that "our wars are done." We hear, and we know, that a scarcely bearable weight of work lies ahead of us, whether we live in an English village or an American city, by the Danube or the Dnieper. But we shall do it best if we do not shut ourselves morbidly off from the blessed power Recreation. "Each man," in his national way, "to what sport and revels his addiction leads him." Kermesse will be king of the castle for certain days or we shall never make up for the past with mighty workings. Indeed, it will be very remarkable if the world does not yield to nature, and express not only its burdens but its joy on the way to better enterprise. About the year 1939 I picked up two books which have been increasingly present to my mind; the first, edited by Henry Vizetelly, was *Paris in Peril*—a chronicle of privations and calamities during 1870 and 1871. The second, which is better known, was *Paris Herself Again*, written a few years afterwards by that prince of journalists in search of the gay hour, George Augustus Sala. These books composing a story with a happy ending have provided me with enough hopefulness and private reply to the gloomy apprehensions which we all have at times of a Europe sunk in hate and despair for a generation. They tell me as well as anything can that nature and time solve hardest riddles; that the peoples will not be left in hell, that the fountains of man's joys and pleasures will flow again, and almost— but not quite—that G. A. Sala will be the special correspondent at every fair and every attraction in the new old Europe.

If travellers like me are charged with an intent to stay with *old* Europe, the charge causes no real pain; mankind is old. His advance is a mixture, and his past is often only a matter of appurtenances and details. Perhaps it is in England that a change has taken place which makes our holiday spirit less mediæval than the festivity elsewhere in Europe. I am no antiquary. I seek the general feeling rather than the curious survivals; and there is a heartiness in some public merrymaking elsewhere which does me good. With an excellent judge [1] of these matters, "I always feel that with the Stuarts this country became sadder but not wiser." A historian of the Merry England which then fell into something of a sadness can convey to us the inner and outer jubilancy of our ancestors, which may now be imagined best from the lingering kermesse and carnival beyond the Channel. J. H. Wylie was not cultivating a wish-fulfilment in the splendid passages of his *Henry IV.* from which my topic may be illuminated for a moment: ". . . But the great diversion of our forefathers was mumming. Give them but free air and an antique guise, and they would mask and mime with all the seriousness of children at play. Every misery must have its riding, and every gild its procession. . . . At Norwich on St. George's Day, they chose their George and a man to bear his sword and be his carver; two of the brethren bore the banner and two "the wax," and the rest rode with them in their livery round the town. . . . On St. Nicholas's Eve (December 5th) the chorister boys of every cathedral, and probably in every collegiate and parish church where singing boys were found, elected one of their number to be their ' Barne-Bishop,' or St. Nicholas Bishop, and to rule the services of the church, in mitre, ring, gloves, cope, surplice, rochet, and full pontificals. He rode or strutted about the streets with his crozier borne before him, blessing the crowd, and collecting their pennies in a glove, with his canons, chaplains, clerks, vergers and candlebearers, till Childermas. Each season brought its ales, its mayings—round-the-shaft, its Piffany mummings, its Candlemas, Hocktide and Yule; but Corpus Christi was the feast of feasts, when the gildsmen carried torches, candles, and banners around the Blessed Sacrament as it passed through the streets, and all the town turned out at sunrise to watch the annual play."

Merry it was—the very word laughs out from our old literature at every turn; and I rejoice that even under present shadows something of the old persuasion may show its

---

[1] See E. L. Guilford, *Sports and Pastimes in the Middle Ages,* 1920.

face. The other day, according to the best authorities, a gentleman who had communicated a claim to the throne of one of the occupied countries of Europe was announced as the speaker at an intellectual society in one of the colleges of—Isisbridge. The younger residents in the college, other than the actual members of the society, when they got wind of the royal advent, were unwilling to let it pass by without a little ceremony. Nothing was specially concerted, no committee met, but a revelry just grew; and when the personage in his peculiar robes arrived and was being escorted by his hosts into the quadrangle, he was hailed by a masked giant, a terrific form (a clever piece of gymnastics by two of the boys behind their own peculiar robes), followed by his A.D.C., and several courtiers carrying banners, namely, fly-papers on sticks, while on both sides the public in cap and gown signified their deference and sense of the occasion. Nor was music wanting,—

Sonorous metal pouring martial sounds;

the chief performers on the brass nozzles of the fire hoses blew loud and long. The King was visibly moved by this reception. His escort, the secretary of the society, was moved too, for he had visions of the King's being suddenly hoisted on lusty shoulders and popped into one of the Static Water Supplies, as they are called; but that rite was not used, and the King's robes remained on his person. However, as it chanced, some practice bombs placed here and there among the old buildings for an exercise of the Fire Guard went off abruptly in fair imitation of the cannon at the court of Hamlet; and throughout the King's address to the elect, a deal of serenading and bomb and nozzle music continued outside,—then all went on duty and the sport was over.

When I look at those entrancing pamphlets and folders on Continental resorts, the issue of which has been interrupted but will one day be resumed, I am informed by almost all that sport of the organised and technically brilliant kinds has been making vast strides in every country. Winter sports apart, this is the kind of thing which we have been receiving, and that it speaks of a world of pleasure and benefit I do not question: "Every form of sport is to be had in France, and many physical culture centres have been set up within the last few years. Most health resorts have *golf-courses*, and indoor or outdoor *tennis courts*. . . . Dog-racing, which is becoming increasingly popular, takes place on the Courbevoie track, just outside Paris. In every region, are held in well-equipped *stadiums* popular athletic events (rugby, association football, etc.). One of the most famous *cycling events* is the " Tour de France, held yearly." But at that name, Le Tour de France, I forget the rest ; it is indeed an athletic contest, but it is a different affair and recalls to me something more like the ancient and gladdening spirit of pastime than the others.

I daresay you have heard of this Tour, which in ordinary times catches the imagination of France in a manner probably beyond that of even a Cup Final or Grand National here. It has the advantage that, lasting four weeks or so, it goes the round of the country, it is everybody's at one point or another, and it exists as the grand highways do in their national unity, and business of life; these cyclists, while they strive for their prize, trace out the glorious map of their land, so various and so single. "The majority of the districts and the great cities are witnesses of one or another phase of the battle; here they see a splendid piece of long-sighted control, there some bright spurt by the son of the soil who knows his own, and further on again a fantastic chase. Deep in the farm country, along the roads of the Alps or the Pyrenees, there is not a villager nor a peasant who fails to follow with enthusiasm the riders as they pass." And then, the Tour is old enough to have its touch of legendary heroisms; before 1914 the names began to be Homeric, and as we may speak of Hirst and S. M. J. Woods and Palairet and J. T. Tyldesley, so they grew fond over Garrigou, and Trousselier, and Petit Breton; and later on

the catalogue justly included Speicher, and Level, and
Archambaud.

The last time that I had a glimpse of this Tour de France,
it was not among the high mountains, nor at a point of
extreme excitement and speculation. Le Mont de Cassel,
however, is a considerable summit in the well-farmed plains
south from Dunkirk, and the beautiful little town with its
life apart, even its language, was as pleasant to me to be in
for such an occasion as any between Brest and Nice could
have been. Its people have seen strange sights, and wars too
many—even the present one has surged over the ancient
Castellum, and to us who idolised alike its delicate graces
and its healthy rusticities the horror of the visitation,
especially as we do not know how things have been going
in the darkness of war, is most bitter. I never witnessed a
simpler happiness, a crowd moved more delightfully by a
"sporting event" or a diversion, than that arising in the
square and the stony streets of Cassel when the cyclists who
were competing all the way round France mounted the
hill. There was no other subject in Cassel for that time;
work had ceased; and the pavements, which are scarcely
more than edges to the cobbled roads, were crowded with
watchers of all ages. Up came the leading riders, and up
went the handkerchiefs and acclamations; with the spirit
of admiration, the familiar and the humorous aspect com-
bined quite easily; the heroes, battling along in the heat,
grinned cordially at all the homely jokes and some ambigu-
ous encouragements roared at them by vinous gentry
pushing out with their friendliness into the roadway. It
was, after all, everybody's game, a development from
ordinary life and habit; when I asked our old head waiter
at that incomparable little inn over in Belgium what he
did on his days off, he answered glowingly, "Je roule dans
la campagne." But perhaps one day we shall have a Tour of
England with as much local and general celebration. We,
too, have our townsfolk who "roulent dans la campagne"
with complete devotion to their deity, the wheel. They

forge away and make their circuits as though no other sport
or byplay existed; I should not like to ask them whether
they thought the West Indians would win the Oval Test,
or anything so remote from them as that. They pursue some
vision which clearly never disappoints them, which excites
no greedy ardours, no envies. It is simple glory—on they
ply, he and she, a dozen perhaps in a drove, exactly dex-
terous, intent, in a world of their own. I cannot omit to
name their former literary representative, "Kuklos," who
at the outbreak of war in 1914 naturally got out his bicycle
and his needments for it, and, landing in France, pedalled
off in the usual manner for a little tour, under the somewhat unusual circumstances.

Nor would I forget those sad men of genius who have
from time to time displayed the ghostly and metaphysical
opposite to the pleasures of the race of "Kuklos." Years have
passed since some friends led the way to the variety programme in which the stars were of too high magnitude for
the proper attention to be given to my private choice: "Sam
Barton. He Nearly Rides a Bicycle." Arrayed woefully,
apparently in the remnants of the gowns of Victorian under-
graduates, this pensive man with hollow mutterings pushed
forth his incredible Velocipede, and it soon became evident
that he was filled with a radiant sense of the heavenly
beauty which should fill his being if he succeeded in riding
it. Yet this attainment proved uncommonly difficult. His
anxiety grew, his gestures and his clamberings became swift
and frantic—various bedevilments attacked the machine, and
the heaven that had glittered so kindly from those handle-
bars became a hell. But O, at last, the bicycle having magi-
cally reconstituted itself in smaller size at last, just for a
moment, heaven vouchsafed to the votary a reward; there
he was, Sam with his black rags and tatters draped gracefully
round his toiling legs, making a little round awheel; almost
over, but still going; seraphic his face, the face of the seer
in his clearest sight of Pisgah, the transcendent one.

XV

Something of the Tail

IN any kind of sport, nothing charms us more than when some one who feared that he should never manage it at all is providentially permitted to get past that stage. Of all the glowing moments in the life of the late Pickwick, surely the richest was on the ice at Dingley Dell, when he obliged Sam Weller and his call, "Keep the pot a-bilin', sir," by taking his turn on the slide with unexpected success. We still "contemplate the playful smile which mantled on his face when he had accomplished the distance, and the eagerness with which he turned round when he had done so, and ran after his predecessor; his black gaiters tripping pleasantly through the snow, and his eyes beaming cheerfulness and gladness through his spectacles." We need not dwell on the catastrophe which was not caused so much by Pickwick's enthusiasm as by his weight, nor call it the work of Nemesis, since we all share his feelings of bliss when we have some similar good fortune in a game we were afraid we could not play in the least. The results may, of course, be alarming, and matter for sermons rather than these pages.

From this human weakness and harmless vanity, we shall nevertheless observe as Mr. Pickwick might how benevolence spreads. I am afraid that the ingenious have observed it for their own purposes. Some time back a team of carefree cricketers, to whose rank I had been temporarily raised, went forth in the early afternoon to a village match, and duly called on their arrival at the house of the Squire on whose ground we were to perform. He showed some alarm at the number and probable appetites and thirst of the visitors, and rather huffily led the way to the ground.

It was found that he was playing himself, but that not being a cricketer in the ordinary course of things, he was batting last. The village side had a dreary time of it, and the Squire's turn with the bat arrived all too soon, after a run of savage success by the visiting bowlers. But I noticed that the bowling became strangely tired and inaccurate on his arrival, and he soon struck one of some slow air-borne deliveries on the leg side to the hedge. "Four runs, that's not so bad," he commented; and mishitting the next ball, he lifted a catch which was let go, the two fieldsmen nearest seeming to be in a misunderstanding—it can happen; another run to the batsman. To cut the story short, the Squire's batting was remarkably successful, and when the innings closed his score of 20 was most warmly applauded by every visitor—a little too warmly, you might have said. But the Squire was in no mood to pry into such a subject: he was in a state of honest delight and he found a word for it in a general call to supper—"We'll scratch up a ham-bone or something, and if you fellows don't mind drinking just beer . . ."—indeed, there was a faultless joint of beef and a drop of Scotch at the finish. May we all imitate the liberality of this fine old Englishman, next time we have been given such an innings in any game—and let us not inquire into the sources of our sudden mastery any more than he did.

The happiest face I ever saw on a cricket ground, the happiest exclamation I ever heard there, belong to a still more distant day of sunshine. Then also my post was behind the stumps, and then also the last batsman (he was about to join the Army for the old war) came to the crease in faultless flannels but without any hope. However, he immediately cracked a yorker served up to him away into the country, and was about to run, but I said, "Don't bother—Boundary." He smiled like a new sun and cried out, "Good Egg!" He repeated the feat, and that, I think, was all, but it was enough. The expression which he used has ceased to be heard, so far as I have noticed, but to me it

will remain the gladdest of all glad phrases—"Good Egg!
—Jolly Good Egg," the only word for that supreme moment.

> "They're all Winners—*all* Winners;
> Except the Losers, why they're ALL Winners."

So the song says; and it is one of the secrets of the great
games that the Losers, the majority of us, are such regular
and valuable performers. We toil on happily, in every corner
of the world, "the hoyps and scraps" upon whom the great
ones base their triumphs; without us where would they be?
We do not grudge them their glories, but we have our
private world in which after all we feel comfortable enough.
The Good Egg occasionally glitters all gold for us there,
and we do not complain because it is not delivered by the
score or the gross. Someone should pay us a juster tribute
than the innumerable cartoons and lampoons that have been
tossed at us as we made our way back from the scene which
we had braved even if we had not adorned. "Did an elderly
gentleman essay to stop the progress of the ball, it rolled
between his legs, or slipped between his fingers. Did a slim
gentleman try to catch it, it struck him on the nose, and
bounded pleasantly off with redoubled violence, while the
slim gentleman's eyes filled with water, and his form writhed
with anguish." That is the manner in which the Loser's
quality is treated in the classical passage on such matters,
but let us sternly reprehend it. One day we shall bowl out
one or two All-Muggletonians, or strike their most tremendous bowling out into the hayfield.

> In Reason's ear we all collect
> More runs than foolish wags expect,
> For ever singing as we shine,
> Not envying Fagg or Constantine.

I have known cricketers who, as far as my observation went,
practically never scored a run, nor were called on to bowl,

nor took much part in the rest of the proceedings; and yet they were always present, always eager. Perhaps they were practising some metaphysical subtlety upon the game and the others in it and round it; but then they never seemed to speak much, so I cannot pretend to have fathomed their ultimate beatitude.

These thoughts on a mystery which is shared by many persons remote from ball games O, by what millions of us who play on pianos and who dabble in paint and who make our after-dinner speeches and write our epics and our sonnet sequences—these lead me back to the British artists and their cricket scenes. Perhaps one will arise at last who is predestined to interpret the play and the players as no painter ever did yet, and who will fill the walls of some pavilion of the future with panel on panel of action, character, crisis in this field. I have heard it said that often a back view of a man may be the best portrait of him; I am as certain that the cricket view of many men would be the one to snatch from the obscuring hurry of the years. Why should the sly wits of the pencil, the Rowlandsons and the Seymours, have it all their own way, and confine our attention to the anti-graces? When we retrace the golden hours of the famous matches (and not only of those), we are aware of the many opportunities which they brought for the artist's capture of the noble energy, the free and bold attitude, the intense outline, the contrast and balance of figures; surely no kermesse, no skirmish, no procession of prelates or grandees ever offered more to the painter of "the vital truth of form." Seen more closely, too, the cricket match is a treasury of individual looks and ways of physical expression, as interesting as any in the world—sunlit, moreover, so long as the season is reasonable, and as candid and spontaneous as the sunlight. Here is a living picture of emotion, here is intellect, with every stage of youth and experience; here for the time the zeal of a man is confessed clearly in its particular style, and no zeal can be more generous and honourable—for cricket has no hidden designs on mankind. The most satirical-faced spin bowler is only an enemy and a malcontent in our common dream. I would have these living cricketana preserved, and greatly preserved, with the sympathy of the genius; and when the man comes, he may even be able to tell us in subtle portraiture what it is that sustains the enthusiasm of the ever unsuccessful player as he comes up afresh for execution, Wednesdays and Saturdays.

XVI

Gargantua Played Cricket

Aᴄᴛᴇʀ his supper, according to the sufficient authority of Rabelais, Gargantua played games, and he played a great many, the catalogue of them includes 214, and though this number is achieved partly by repetitions of the same game under more than one title, still, Gargantua after supper washed his hands in wine and had variety of games —as great variety as they say the young princes of antiquity had. What all these curious titles meant in practice may be left to the small print of the commentaries, for we must think of many of them as being more in the nature of chimerical possibilities than recoverable accomplishments; the English translators have almost beaten their original in the humour of it. To name but one instance, what could be the rules of "Fair and Softly Passeth Lent"? Yet these translators have not denied to Gargantua some games that exist in the light of day, and he plays in the intervals of the unknown or unknowable ones "at the chess," "at the tric trac" (so did young William Wordsworth with Mr. Charles Lamb), "at the billiards," "at the quoits," and even "at cricket."

They say that much of remote worship and ceremonial, of the wisdom of the ancients, of history that has gone into darkness, of once usual manners and customs, is concealed within the games that children play still and the rhymes that they sing.

> Through what wild centuries
> Roves back the rose;

and Gargantua playing at cricket was probably no better

informed on the symbolism of his game than we are now. It may have been conceived by some religious layman as a variation on the old theme of good and evil in contest, white spirits and black; a popular extension of the dramatic forms in which this holy war was seasonally set before the community. The virtuous soul, resisting the deadly sins, militant against the hosts of the prince of darkness, might be the type of more than a show and spectacle; might be enacted with fortitude and vigilance by the young men who possibly tended to drift away from the high imagery on the players' platform in the market-place. Any batsman will agree that the natural bias of batsmen is towards magnanimity and beauty of soul, whereas that of bowlers sets sedulously towards malice and uncharitableness—even their appearances of sympathy are full of guile—and this class of beings is leagued with encircling fieldsmen of a similar predatory purpose; above all, there is one, a wicket-keeper, lurking ever behind, practically invisible, heavily armed, "shedding influence malign." Then, there are several ways of getting out, enough to make almost the best of batsmen mutter from his Omar those lines, a little damaged:

> Oh, Thou, who didst with Pitfall and with Gin
> Beset me, under orders to stay in
> At least, if not to score, till stumps are drawn,
> Surely Thou canst not have conspired with Sin?

Another allegorical design has been propounded in this matter of cricket by one who reads the Sonnets of Shakespeare in the hope of discovering whether or not the author was a left-hander. This observant man paused over the verses, which have held so many in thrall:

> Oh, how shall summer's honey breath hold out
> Against the wreckful siege of battering days,

and he had a new idea. These verses seemed to disclose the

inwardness of the cricket morality: here, in this game, an anonymous poetic inventor had represented the inevitable fate of loveliness, high endeavour and charm. The notion was strengthened by what he had been growing accustomed to, in some Test Matches of the period: by the sort of casualty list among batsmen which might run thus:

> Hobbs, c. and b. Mailey - - 11
> Sutcliffe, b. Gregory - - 27
> Hendren, b. Gregory - - 0

and so on. Agreed that the evidence was not on every occasion quite so clearly on the side of his theory:

> Bardsley, run out - - - 79
> Armstrong, c. Hobbs, b. Woolley 81
> Macartney, b. Braund - - 123

. . . In such instances, the game had obviously departed from the intentions of the founder, who had scarcely predicted any such well-trained pitches as we play on even in the village of Bumpdown Goliath, enabling individual players to stay at the crease for periods of thirty and even sixty minutes.

The resolute decipherers of figurative creations, the translator of myths who perhaps has agreed with the tracing of the Book of Revelation to folk-memory of a collision between an elder Moon and this long-suffering Earth, will surely unfold one day the common experience wrapt so long within the Laws of Cricket and the game and play. I do not uphold those theories which I noted above. It will be enough to observe the competition of these and others in days when we have room and verge enough for these peaceful adventures. Some will then tell me that the secret is no more than a straightforward weather masque of "summer's honey breath," of the season (as we know it in England particularly) contending with the east winds and nipping frosts, and presently glowing forth into a triumph which might seem eternal. There is indeed a sunshine within the game when we witness some prolonged display of its rich detail, supposing that the period of caution and doggedness and reserved intention has been got over. Some, seeking a wider solution, may view the whole thing as a speculum of the game of life, with success and unsuccess, with the reward of merit but the intrusion of chance, with loneliness and with company, with romance and common-place, with the dispute of the fine touch and the fierce assault—and in midst of all the mind and spirit of man, ever striving "rightly to be great."

Perhaps I have fallen into a strain rather more ambitious and more intricate than I foresaw I might, and it is certain that it would not be greeted with applause if I were to begin speaking in this manner while the pads are being put on next Wednesday. We shall be on our best prosaic behaviour. There will be no metaphysical batsmen, and bowlers who insist on being symbolical or folk-lorish will not be given a second over. From my usual post I shall observe those realistic Individual Scores which certain batsmen inscribe on the backs of their bats. And yet at any moment something of the deeper life may come over the game and may modify and deepen the feelings of all who take part in it. A stand by the last wicket pair, for example—when the innings had appeared quite remorselessly broken down, and No. 11 came to the crease amid a general intimation of the pathetic and the irrelevant. But should he and the worn and anxious man at the other end dig in for a little, and still a little, and still some more, and then begin to look round for the gaps in the field and flash out some strokes in the spirit of art as though they had half a dozen crack batsmen to follow them in the event of a misjudgment, why then we shall all be reminded that there is a romance, there may be a parable in what had just now looked a flattish kind of game. And perhaps I shall take comfort and quote to some-body (hardly the umpires, who have watched many miracles over those well-planted boots) the appreciation of this particular type of partnership which no less a philosopher than George Meredith has uttered—in *The Match of Fallowfield against Beckley* which is played in the story of *Evan Harrington*. (I infer from that chapter that George Meredith used to be sent in to bat at the end of the tail.) "The two last men of an eleven are twins: they hold one life between them; so that he who dies extinguishes the other. Your faculties are stirred to their depths. You become engaged on the noblest of rivalries; in defending your own, you fight for your comrade's existence. You are assured that the dread of shame, if not emulation, is making him equally wary and alert."

And if this specimen of cricketology tempts someone to ask for more, and if the last pair continue to enjoy good luck and mix it with good play, then Meredith may still protect me with this august example: "The field took breath with the heroes; and presume not to doubt that heroes they are. It is good to win glory for your country; it is also good to win glory for you village. A Member of Parliament, Sir George Lowton, notes this emphatically, from the statesman's eminence, to a group of gentlemen on horseback round a carriage wherein a couple of fair ladies reclined. 'They didn't shout more at the news of the Battle of Waterloo. Now this is our peculiarity. . . .'" After which, I think only the voice of the Countess in the story should be heard, and perhaps she is a little hard on us and our mystery: "You can cricket, and you can walk, and will very soon learn how to give your arm to a lady. I have hopes of you."

Were I to be sent forth as in an earlier page I fancied E. V. L. going in the world of shades, to gather their additions to what they have left in writing among us living, I should hardly resist asking some of them for amplifications valuable to my present thoughts. Perhaps they would beg to be excused from going into the matter, and I might have to console myself with the brief things that they formerly said; calling those brevities, with as much conviction as I could, "a volume in a word," or some such comforting phrase. In spite of that I should like to hear more from John Keats in elucidation of a passage which he wrote in 1818 to his brother George in "the Western wild"—Hear this, citizens of Louisville!—and which surely covers a multitude of cogitable things: "I should wish to give you a picture of our Lives here whenever by a touch I can do it even as you must see by the last sentence our walk past Whitehall all in good health and spirits—this I am certain of, because I felt so much pleasure from the simple idea of your playing a game at Cricket." I should ask Shelley why, when he mentions roundness in some philosophical sense, he chooses a cricket ball as an illustration. I should beg W. M. Thackeray, too, who will not have forgotten Fableland, to say something on the wealth of his meanings or his feelings behind one or two minute details in *The Newcomes*. They belong to the career, to the personality of the beloved Colonel, who we recall was fairly bewildered by hearing "that young Keats was a genius to be estimated in future days with young Raphael," and who tried without success to fathom this by wading through *Lamia*; but it is not the Colonel's literary experience which I have now most in mind. It is something earlier and later, and easier and happier, in his world. That affair of his running away from home in childhood, to begin with; concluding in the apparition of his father, horsewhip in hand, in the cottage bedroom: "Tommy, scared out of a sweet sleep and a delightful dream of cricket, knew his fate." And to end with, ages afterwards, the Colonel on his deathbed: "One afternoon he asked for his little gown-boy, and the child was brought to him, and sat by the bed with a very awe-stricken face; and then gathered courage, and tried to amuse him by telling him how it was a half-holiday, and they were having a cricket-match with the St. Peter's boys in the green, and Grey Friars was in and winning. The Colonel quite understood about it; he would like to see the game; he had played many a game on that green when he was a boy. He grew excited. . . ."

Surely this was a hinted history of Thackeray's own delightful dream, and understanding, and excitement; and if after all it was the age of childhood that stirred him more than the particular pastime, still the world which he drew was a child world throughout. Perhaps he did not choose cricket as the example of the best juvenile pleasures, and so of all, without a portion of "those characteristic and recurrent thoughts which passed through that grave brain." I am sorry in such a case that we have not more of them; unkind Thackeray for once, to have written so marvellous a collection of roundabout papers, and not the one that would have enriched the finer criticism of our game. And if I am to complain, *only once*, against this glorious lover of life and master of the humour of it, now is the time to grudge the placing of the sacred implements, a bat and a set of stumps, in the hamlike hand of—Duval the Pirate, drawn with force by Mr. Michael Angelo Titmarsh among the personages in *Dr. Birch and his Young Friends*. But to mention that is almost enough to set me off on a panegyric of Thackeray the artist, and that again on Thackeray the critic of artists, and indeed on a book which would almost weigh as much as that ivied tomb at Kensal Green, and perhaps be as little frequented.

Whatever may have been the morality play which was shaped out as cricket, or if after all explorings it is declared scientifically that there was none at all in the minds of the improvisors—only one of those impulses which still rise up even in the severest stages of a Test Match, to clout a ball harder and higher than Nature had ordained—it is now as rich in psychological combat and curiosity as any game can be. It has the essential virtue of never quite repeating itself. Like the art of poetry it is ever just a little different from what it has been, moving on without saying that it does so, freshening and hastening and curving without clamorous quarrel over its yesterdays. If some violent novelty be suddenly thrown into it, the gods are seen to avert their faces from the show, and then there is a clamour whence before long the right degree of reconsideration will have been accepted. I wonder what would happen if someone should invent a ball, for brightening cricket, which did tricks unknown to our "popular makes." I think it and possibly its manufacturer would be burned at Lord's in the presence of the most illustrious company ever gathered even there, not to mention the usual host of us who try to pass the turnstiles six at a time when something is stirring.

And nobody knows who it was that first made a ball, and thereby made cricket and some other games which Gargantua played and a vast number which he did not. Call him Merlin—but that clever rogue must have been too late for the priority. A suspicion also arises that the ball can hardly have been a British invention. It is with a sense of shame that I remember casting a careless eye on the extraordinary collection of balls of all nations, materials, sizes, purposes, presented by Mr. T. H. Oyler to the museum at Maidstone; for that was a moment due to veneration and wonder, as when we first realise something of the wardrobe of Queen Elizabeth. Perhaps the Oyler collection did not include a Balloon, which, short of the grand terrestrial ball and others similar but larger, may be held to be the most dignified form of all these orbs and rondures; I have been told that it also provides the finest sport or pastime which any of them do—but the balloonist who held this opinion had really failed as a cricketer. Besides, he was designed by nature for the air, or in the words of Martin F. Tupper:

with energetic elasticity to leap the gulfs of contrast.

I have a dim recollection that the Balloon Races of the late nineteenth century were not such successful events as was hoped; but to speak of this other Mystery from the outside, and from the ground which I have never much wished to leave, is reckless. At least a hero-worship of the balloonists of all times has been part of me as long as I can recall, and I have a special affection for those who, when the dreams that the balloon would be a tremendously practical piece of human equipment had faded away, made a name and spent the prime of their lives as sportsmen with the great toy. The names?—Captain Graham, Mrs. Graham, Captain Currie, the Marquis of Clanricarde; I remember no more, at least of those who flourished and flew in the reign of George IV. And later Charles Green. These and many more played at ball in the clouds when the world was younger, and in their eyes I can see a light which does not die.

And yet (for not all could say what Mrs. Graham once heard from Captain Currie in his balloon, "Oh, Mrs. Graham! let us never return to earth!") the use of a ball in something nearer village-shop sizes attracts, and the green field and the limited arena compel, and it may not be cynical to guess that—

Fives does more than Zeppelin can
To justify God's ways to man.

The big-scale sports, perhaps, are lacking in fundamental brainwork. Their equipment is astounding, their power is staggering—and they are rather dull. I might have been induced once to pay my denarii and sit on my stone bench watching the lions issue from their tunnel and the Christians from theirs—but it would have been the last time. Those colossal orgies of angling for fish like 4000-pound bombs which I have only seen at the pictures appal me, and numb me; the bloodstreaked battle between the terrible and cunning sea-monsters and the inflexible and ingeniously furnished humans who have hooked them to their relentless rods is not my idea of a summer's joy. Much more intriguing is the slow fellow with his float and bit of weed on the hook, hoping for one of the roach who have been studying the art of angling under the weir since leaves were green. I have yet to consult a Toreador on the hidden graces and intellectual pleasures of his profession, but I cannot help thinking that it is "monotonous for the bull" and dependent on emotions which need not be added to what we have to bear.

The dictionary of sports and pastimes, an extensive one, yields but few that are universally followed; golf, lawn tennis, football appear to be those, other than pure athletics, which are sooner or later to be the games of all countries. I cannot yet notice the signs that baseball or cricket will become as native everywhere as these have been doing. It was long ago remarked that the extent of the British Empire will be reconstructed by the experts of some later civilisation through the exhuming of fossilised bats and balls. Meanwhile, in the next great Atlas to be produced by English map-makers (and it is said that the time for one is ripe, subject to a year or two of peace) a map of the distribution of games through the world might be included. The inferences to be drawn from it are not within my power to draw; but they might be curious. The Japanese, who have kept themselves free from cricket in spite of their long tradition of English studies, are a nation of baseball-players; they have rushed into a war with the mighty country which they attempt to emulate in this and some other respects. Something of fantasy and overstrain underlies this paradoxical and costly outbreak. The English have from time to time been cajoled into a willingness to let baseball find a home among them; it does not. The finest demonstrations are given, pass by, and the situation remains unchanged. Formerly the Americans (like Keats's American brother) had some room for cricket, and the name of J. B. King of the *Gentlemen of Philadelphia* is treasured yet by old admirers here; but the tradition has declined, and it would be a bold man who would predict that it could ever spring again. But who will have the confidence to assert even that Australia fifty years hence will be principally a cricket-playing nation? It seems their luck that they can have both baseball and cricket according to the season. At least we may be sure that Australia will be playing something.

May that something still be cricket! How beautifully they have played it, and how they have kept it young! I am reminded that I have never set eyes on an old Australian; presumably they have some of this description, and my friend Wag who has taken the wicket of Victor Richardson more than once insists on having a baldness on his head at a still early age, which almost makes him of the race of Perkin Warbeck. The other day, at an advanced age, died Ernest Jones, once Australia's fast bowler, and the most furious of his line. It is said that he ever maintained one side of his moustache yellow, while the other was grey—a colourful defiance of the years. But, in the freer and more reasonable spirit of truth, the Australians are young and communicate youth; and their charm as they field out, and fling the ball about, and even dance a little in the most austere conditions (I remember Fleetwood-Smith in the Oval catastrophe which preceded the War) has been "sung so oft and oft" that I am without the next words to suggest it. That is only one aspect. Indeed my statement is impeccable, except for:

(1) W. W. Armstrong. I believe that he is the predestined Oldest Cricketer, except Dr. Grace, who ever drew the attention of all ranks to the proper width of a bat.

(2) W. J. O'Reilly. But I conjecture that his presentment of Eternity is only a mask to accompany his innumerable overs.

XVII

Spirit of the Game

A CHARM of cricket and its days in the sun dwells and will dwell in the names of clubs which have been honoured throughout England and wherever the game is known; amateur societies, which surely came into being under a poetic inspiration, tempered duly with regard for the common sense of sport and pastime. Of all these now extant the I Zingari came first. You would think that George Borrow must have been the secretary. I don't know if their password would be *Ducdame*—"What's that Ducdame?" —but there is all the breeze and glow of June in their title. These titles float up in my mind like glittering clouds over the broad breasts of the Downs; they are such as command permanence. The Free Foresters!

> In summertime when shaws be green,
> And leaves be large and long . . .

Robin Hood's cricket is uncertain, owing to the carelessness of his balladists; but we have in the mention of these celebrated spirits a portion of his genius. Or better still, some touch of Shakespeare; since in reality their forest is the Forest of Arden. The Blue Mantles! but for these I must ever have a special regard, since once they included the truest poet-cricketer of our day, and not from a zest on the part of the Club for verse but for a union of qualities—one whom I have mentioned before, S. S.

These with others could almost be noted down into a cricket poem, a pastoral, just as the memory awakens: the Band of Brothers, the Invalids, the Hampshire Hogs, the Devon Dumplings, Harlequins, Authentics, Barnacles,

Perambulators, Incogniti, Wanderers, Yellowhammers, Grasshoppers, Quidnuncs, Sussex Martlets, Somerset Stragglers, Derbyshire Friars, Brighton Brunswick, Thespids, Stoics, Cryptics, Cyphers, Nondescripts—but perhaps some other pen will find the right musical order in which they ought to appear. As for their cricket order, it matters little here; "their importance is" one and the same, and it is not like some of the importances which confront our world, harsh and assertive, but as unassuming as the daisies which will not be banished from the grounds on which these cricketers are seen to advantage. From these clubs the cricket world receives a constant influence, and those of us who will scarcely ever rise to the dignity of playing in a match against one of them, those of us who may never have chanced to see one of them play, feel that the influence is a breath of life to the game throughout. It is a style, a chivalry, a distinction. By its workings the freedom of cricket is kept safe and sound; not only by this one type of amateur excellence, of course—yet the poetry and philosophy of the names carries a fine significance throughout the field of play which geographers may mark from Easter Island perhaps to Copenhagen. It is delightful to be playing for *our* village when word goes about that among our visitors there is one with a cap revealing that he is of one of these gentlemanly clubs; now he is batting, and we are taken at once with the manner of it all—it may bring about our overthrow, we know what we are in for if he stays, and yet if he goes we shall not be so violently pleased. The words to the crossing fieldsmen, the glance round the picture which the ground gives, the affectionate examining of the bat after some slight chance that it was not perfectly happy, the modest studious downward look after a series of classic strokes to the off boundary and then a glide to the other—these attend such cricketers. These too are players who keep the game young. In other fields, where the bowling is literally deadly, they equally with the Australians defy age.

A light like theirs is never unnecessary in the continuance of a game with such tremendous business aspects as cricket. We have seen how mightily organised it becomes and what grimness may and must enter into it when the notion of a business gets the upper hand of its old lyrical element. A century or nearly one has elapsed since I Zingari first wandered into the world, and as all cricketers are indebted to them for coming into being and will be able to remain true cricketers in part through that fact, I will transcribe the characteristic circumstances of their origin.

> They dreamed not of a perishable fame
> Who thus could build:

but they dreamed. Here is the story, already a time-honoured one in 1863; from *London Society* of that year it appears that:

"When once you throw great men together, something greater is ever likely to sparkle and bubble forth. Accordingly 'one day in the month of July, 1845,' *vera loquor*, F. Ponsonby, S. Ponsonby, R. P. Long and I. L. Baldwin, good men and true, finding themselves at supper at the Blenheim Hotel, then and there formed a club, christened the same, framed rules, and the following day informed twenty-one of their friends that they had received the distinguished honour of being members of I Zingari. That there is something truly pure-minded and disinterested in this community, the slightest glance at their laws will prove. With all other societies the first thing you hear is, 'Pay your money;' but with the Zingari, Rule 6 relieves your apprehension, thus—'That the entrance be nothing, and that the annual subscription do not exceed the entrance.' Nevertheless, though the Zingari treasury does not contain as much as shin plaster, it is duly protected by two secretaries, one chancellor, one liberal legal adviser, and one treasurer and auditor of their financial accounts. . . . As they savour of such remote antiquity, it were long to trace the achievements and the distinguished honours of the Zingari. . . . Their principle has been to provide the best of amateur play . . . and their numbers are annually recruited from the rising talent of the day—as they enact *si bene se gesserint*, meaning, probably, what is written up in some village schools, ' None admitted that don't learn manners.'"

And so, to-day, this club and its many successors and rivals provide a kind of elixir for our game. But another and more telling metaphor has been given us by Sir Home Gordon: "English cricket may be compared to an imposing edifice. The spacious foundations are formed by village matches. On that is raised the charming ground-floor of club cricket. The more austere and less irresponsible super-structure of county encounters appears majestic but severe. The cupola consists of Test Matches and is so elevated as to excite ambitious aspirations, but also so bleakly exposed as to lose recreative consciousness." Who will not linger in rapt contemplation of this beautiful delineation of the fabric of cricket? It merits comparison with nothing less than Samuel Taylor Coleridge's many word-castles illus-trating his view of "The constitution of Church and State," and probably it has discovered a larger number of more attentive readers.

Take away the breezy impulses of the club cricket so interpreted to us, and the outlook darkens; a gloom sits on the horizon, and I can almost see in the consequence the abandonment of the game altogether or rather of the game's by-product. A fable of historic instance which happened in my way as I was reading the *Letters of Pliny* and of which the recorder professed himself unable to point out the application, has been disturbing me. I apprehend that it might apply to the misdirection and disproportioning of the best of games. But here is Pliny's story as well as I can paraphrase it: There used to be a town in Africa called Hippo, which stood on a great lake a few miles from the sea and joined to the sea by a river. This lake was vastly popular with boys of all ages, who used to throng to it for fishing, sailing, swimming and all the water-sports. The boys who were as yet only beginners at shaving came to it for a famous swimming competition, the object of which was simply to swim out farthest; and no doubt it required alike skill, and judgment, and courage. One day a boy thought that he would make for the opposite shore, as he had left his comrades well behind; and while he was about it, a dolphin came along, and frolicked round him. He was scared, but the dolphin was obviously friendly, and presently took him on his back, and was so obliging as to carry him across the lake again and land him among his mates.—Even Captain Webb never managed this, and Charles Waterton's ride on a crocodile was comparatively brief.

To continue: our dolphineer was quickly the centre of a crowd of excited people asking questions and expanding the answers, and the whole town was soon talking of the performance. Next day it seemed to have shut up all its affairs and congregated at the lake side, where the lucky lads were once more stripping for their swim. The youth who had been a principal cause of the excitement went in with them, but as we can understand he was rather more cautious this time. Not so the affable dolphin. He soon came to the surface close to the bobbing heads and flashing arms, and showed all his art, springing and plunging and darting and wheeling; and this he did day after day, until the crowd grew familiar with him, whistled and bawled at him to come to the shore, touched and stroked him. Above all, the boy whom he had first addressed and assisted became his intimate companion, and the two were regularly seen swimming side by side, or the boy would be travelling on the back of the fish, while the other youths cheered them on. When the dolphin had played his innings and the boys theirs, he would come up on the shore, roll himself in the sand, enjoy the sunshine, and when he felt like it roll back into his lake and private life.

These happenings came to the notice of the deputy

governor of the province, a good-natured but pompous dignitary, who set a high value on ceremonies, and who made up his mind that the dolphin ought to be honoured as an almost sacred institution. Statues of the gods were anointed, with all due form, in that part of the world; the dolphin should therefore be publicly recognised in the same manner. Accordingly Avitus, with his own hands but at the cost of the state, performed the rite one day upon the dolphin as he was lying on the sands in modest reflections. The precious ointment, however, had an opposite effect to that which Avitus had expected; instead of the dolphin making the equivalent of a speech in acknowledgment of the unmerited marks of public approbation, etc., he wrinkled his nose miserably at the unmarine smell of the stuff, and made off for the waters as fast as he could go, where he remained concealed for several days.

At last he reappeared; a triumphant shout went up from the boys, "There's old Bouncer! there he comes"; but as he drew near it was apparent that he had not liked the ceremony of the scented grease at all. He looked dull and languid but he did his best, and at length felt sufficiently well to give some of those fascinating displays which had formerly won him popularity. These indeed swelled his fame still more, and brought Mayors and Corporations and other officials from distant parts, as spectators of his and the boys' brilliant matches. But the accommodation, and the means, of the little town were sorely strained by the reception of these notables; and over and above that the orderly life and usual arrangements of the community were constantly in a chaos.

Poor dolphin! He went on dutifully doing what he had at first done out of sheerest love of sport and play, and trying to keep his old spirit, together with the affection of his early water-companions, under the restraint of having to break all his own records every day of the week and to learn new tricks for the solace of the many-headed beast with the thunderous throats which wanted him to do other things besides his swimming and leaping. But his release was approaching, though he did not know it. One day the boys were horrified to find him on the shore in his usual place—motionless, mangled, dead. Who killed the dolphin?

Let us return from this sad scene, and leave any application of it that may have seemed the correct one (for there could be several), and drive off any faintest fears that may have been skulking round the back of our cricket pavilion, and think a fond moment longer of the sweetness and light that are ever being found, and ever imparted, in this game. It is not too late to call it gentlemanly, surely; of its best figures it can always be written at length, when they have been statistically enshrined in the memorial section of *Wisden's Almanack*, "His life was gentle." I have never seen their contribution to the game resented by the simpler school of players, by all of us who form our ideals somewhere in the wilderness. Perhaps they are our modern instances of those noble creatures who in the Elizabethan and Caroline periods were instructed along the lines of Peacham's *Compleat Gentleman* and Milton's *Tractate on Education*, though the sports pages of those grave dissertations do not touch on cricket. Not from there did the Victorian headmaster discover the infallible secret for reforming indiscipline in his charges which is described so prettily by a contemporary of his: "Work thrived under so zealous a teacher, and a civilised out-of-door life, in the form of cricket, football and wholesome sports, took the place of poaching, rat-hunting, and poultry-stealing."

From the same period I glean an anecdote which might enrage somebody who reads it on a sudden. "An old family servant was umpiring in a match in which his master's son was playing. Off the very first ball delivered to the latter, an appeal for leg-before-wicket was made. 'How's that, umpire?' shouted the bowler. 'Not hout,' responded that worthy sturdily; adding, however, in a stage whisper, 'If you does that again, Master 'Arry, I really must give you hout!'" Now this feudal tale, at first glance looks black, I

must confess, against Old Family Servant. He is no demo-
crat, nothing but a hireling.—But have we the full history?
I doubt it, as in most instances of remarkable sayings: "I
had rather have written that poem, Gentlemen, than taken
Quebec," or "Be a good man, Lockhart." (About the last,
consult Sir Herbert Grierson's *Life of Scott*, or do not if you
would rather keep a noble illusion.) I can perceive in the
presence of mind shown by O.F.S. a natural longing that
Master 'Arry, a probable Free Forester in the making, should
not be sent to his account so abruptly but permitted to
stay and divert the onlooker with some of his qualities
personal and technical. In fact, the story falls into the class
of those, and they are many, in which umpires of incalcul-
able virtue refused the most confident appeals against W. G.
Grace (in country games) for the public good. As one of
them may have said to the young bowler who had cleaned
up the champion's wicket with a nailer as soon as he came
in, and been hoarsely no-balled a shade after the event, "You
look out what you're a-doing; people haven't come here
to see you bowl but to watch the Doctor bat."

The following heroic couplets, which bear all the marks
of having been composed during the eighteenth century,
were extracted by me from a forlorn and plundered book
of receipts for banishing the vapours and making sugar of
roses.

A Cricket Advice

'Tis not alone the Notches that accrue,
My Son, in Cricket's noble Game, to you,
Nor tale of Wickets by your Art bowl'd down
Which shall your Name among your Fellows crown.
Success, I grant, is much, and vig'rous Play
With Cunning mixt must mark a Conqu'ror's Way;
For who can doubt, the farther driv'n the Ball,
The more the Runs? but Totals are not all.
It must be still our Aim to beat the Bat
When our Opponents take their Turns with that,

And yet our Victory will be dearly gain'd
Were nothing of more lasting Worth attain'd.
Be this your Counsel then: Succeed with Grace,
And should you fail, fail with a gen'rous Face;
Inquire what more than Runs your Bat may give,
For when the Runs are past, the Style may live;
Express a happy Chance in ev'ry Stroke,
Nor like some Spinster at the small Coals poke;
Be fair in Bowling, just to Life and Limb,
The Batsman's Knuckles still belong to him,
And all admire his Downfall caus'd by Thought
Rather than Terror by fast Bumpers wrought.
When fielding out, although the Task be dry,
Still watch the Game with sharp yet loving Eye;
Pursue the fleeting Orb as Hounds the Hare, ⎫
And when the fierce Hit flies into the Air ⎬
With merry Manner risk your Fingers there. ⎭
Deny no Praise even if 'tis at your Cost,
A Match that makes for Friendship is well lost,
And Consolation to th' unlucky speak,
Which you yourself may wish another Week.
E'en lend your Bat, and if it come back chipped,
Betray no slightest Hint of being hipp'd,
And thus in all observe that Cricket grows
Not out of mere Results as some suppose
But from sweet Temper, equable Address,
Friendship with Fortune, handy Willingness;
As when the Gods on bright Olympus met——

From that point I am obliged to say that the poetry has been
consumed by mice, but the author had made his meaning
sufficiently clear: I trust that this will not be too much
against him at the present time. From the handwriting it
appears that he composed his lines in advanced age and with
feelings of a testamentary gravity.

XVIII

The Subject Continued

So the spirit of cricket has drawn me into the eighteenth century and the poetry of that age; and while I am there a poet of very different calibre from my homely rhymer of wisdom at the wicket appears to challenge all of us who believe in the deeper meaning of a game. It is Thomas Gray, and the human generosity of his Elegy makes it hard that he should have implied the sneer at a summer diversion if nothing more, in the following: "There is my Lord Sandwich and Halifax, they are Statesmen: Do not you remember them dirty boys playing at cricket?" To do him justice, Gray included, although he was cautious in his terms, a reference to cricket in that very noble and original *Ode on a Distant Prospect of Eton College*:

> Say, Father THAMES, for thou hast seen
>> Full many a sprightly race
> Disporting on thy margent green
>> The paths of pleasure trace,
> Who foremost now delight to cleave
> With pliant arm thy glassy wave?
>> The captive linnet which enthrall?
> What idle progeny succeed
> To chase the rolling circle's speed,
>> Or urge the flying ball?

Hoops or cricket, it was much the same; and so his allusion does not much improve his position, nor can I read without a pleasure the comment of Dr. Johnson on this stanza: "His supplication to Father Thames, to tell him who drives or tosses the ball, is useless and puerile. Father Thames has no better means of knowing than himself." The spirit of cricket is thumpingly avenged, and from Johnson's technical accuracy here and elsewhere I conjecture that the vengeance was taken by a cricketer.

But then not every one, not even a student of this mortal life as sincere as Gray, can be expected to have the insight of Mr. Robertson-Glasgow into this game, or any other. Another eighteenth-century voice, and a terribly clear and pursuing voice it is, challenges again. "My father, as you have observed, had no great esteem for my uncle Toby's HOBBY-HORSE; he thought it the most ridiculous horse that ever gentleman mounted; and indeed, unless my uncle Toby vexed him about it, could never think of it once, without smiling at it." And yet, I cannot accept all at once that the subject which has produced these chapters is only a Hobby-Horse. It is too old, too generally beloved, too complex and too full-blooded for such a limited relationship. It sprang from the meadows in which I first tasted sorrel and disconcerted a hedgehog who owned the property, and if it be true that it is of a kind not to be really comprehended except by those who came to it in childhood, it is probable that early associations may make up for an imperfect comprehension in those. Or else they have created something visionary, better than a Hobby-Horse; and I willingly believe that this happens in all sorts of affairs, serious or sporting (to allow that distinction). I notice "something visionary" in the zeal of even the toughest Army instructor, expounding his bit of machinery to the raw students; it is a way they have, a way every man has in respect of some particular knowledge and use. On this account the titles which we see on some books for younger readers delight me: I mean those on the pattern, *The Romance of the Post Office*, or *The Romance of the Typewriter*.

Without this special gusto, this personal possession and being-possessed, a great deal that goes on in the world and beguiles a host of our fellow-men is inevitably lost upon us. We make perhaps a nodding acquaintance with it, but it cannot get very far. It resembles the meeting between Sir Walter Scott and Thorwaldsen the Danish sculptor, whose statue of Byron remains at Trinity College, Cambridge; it resembles this too only if we are doing our best. The novelist and the sculptor left to themselves had no common language, and were obliged to express their mutual admiration by looking it; the expression was as warm as it could be under the circumstances, but it could not be continued to any great length or in any minuteness of discussion, though we are told that as they closed the interview—and that is just what it was—they followed each other with their eyes "as long as possible." So it must be, whatever our desire to see through the eyes of others, in many matters of traditions, associations, personal endeavours. It was not vanity in Thomas Gray, to call him up again and this time with all reverence, when he prefixed to some poems requiring a certain scholarly familiarity with some other poems from ancient Greece, that Greek motto signifying, "These are spoken to those of like mind."

When Henry James, in his earlier days, ventured to Epsom and the Derby, he did not go without preliminary training of a sort. He was well assured that this was "the most characteristic of national holidays" in England, and more widely that such events were in England rather big things. "The space allotted to sporting intelligence in a compact, eclectic, 'intellectual' journal like the *Pall Mall Gazette*, had seemed to me for some time past a measure of the hold of such questions upon the British mind." He did not come back from the day with the name of the winner in his memory, an omission which accords with his finding his fun in observing the manners and customs of the crowd; and he sums up the action which had been so eagerly awaited with enviable brilliance. "Seeing the race is indifferent entertainment. If I might be Irish on the occasion of a frolic, I would say that in the first place you do not see it at all, and in the second place you perceive it to be not much worth the seeing. It may be very fine in quality, but in quantity it is inappreciable. . . . The whole sixty thousand are suddenly resolved into unanimity by the sight of a dozen small jockey-heads whizzing along a very distant sky-line. In a shorter space of time than it takes me to write this, the whole thing is before you, and for the instant it is anything but beautiful. A dozen furiously revolving arms—pink, green, orange, scarlet, white—whacking the flanks of as many straining steeds; a glimpse of this, and the spectacle is over." Dangerous as it may be to admit it, I do admit that this impression on the part of Henry James is much the same as mine on similar occasions, and he has written it down without a hitch. But it is evident that Henry James was sent on earth to write *The Aspern Papers* and *The Coxon Fund* rather than a horse-race and the turf; and were one of my old acquaintances from the Newmarket train and inn to put forth his impression even of the spectacle, not to mention his story of all that was passing within its leading or not leading personalities, I am fairly certain that it would be considerable in quantity and rousing in curious inimitable truth.

Had Henry James been living and had he chanced to turn over the pages of this book, I can hardly hope that he would have been moved by its most fortunate persuasions (if there are any) to see cricket through the eyes of the cricketers of Rye or the rest of Sussex, and England, and the British Empire. Hoyle's *Games*, that scientific work, born in 1742 and not easily avoided in the world of books, would stand as much chance—it dealt originally with Whist, but the Laws of Cricket crept in. I wonder if even Nyren, or Mr. Robertson-Glasgow, with all potency of their knowledge of men and language and the profundities of cricket, could have allured the novelist into a fuller seeing of a cricket match than of the race which was just a colour-print on fire. They say that any of us who will talk of what is his own enthusiasm and mastery may soon capture the interest of his hearers. I can only claim the enthusiasm, and yet it may be of some value when a member of the millions who have unwittingly scored a four off the edge in the opposite direction to what was intended makes a small speech on the reasons for his not retiring yet.

For without concealing his wilderness of ignorance concerning most of the games that a modern Gargantua might play, presumably before supper, a close follower of this one might be forgiven for seeing in its organisation a nervous, philosophical, characteristical variety surpassing any of the others. He could appeal to the extant literature upon it, and a bibliography so vast that an item like the present is like another ear of corn in a threshing machine. Apart from field sports, this literature is surely unique. He could quote the Clerk of the Weather, who from Jove's court can and does intervene perhaps half a dozen times in the course of a great match, compelling a whole series of new thought and fresh stratagem, disturbing all kinds of infirmity that it was hoped to shield, mixing the tragical with the comical, to a degree that even Jove's minister cannot reach in any other of our pastimes below.

If the writer on so elemental and so diversified a game as this cannot hope to do more than win a passing glance from those who were not in the secret from the beginning, he has to contend with his fears touching those who were. Tennyson compared poetry to shot silk, its colours glancing differently to different observers; and cricket has the same property. But I conclude that as our experience of it grows into the later decades, it reveals a beauty of temper and outlook which excels all its other actions and passions, and seems to the majority of us to be their flower. A veteran whom I know, quite a non-mystic, who has watched as well as played in a multitude of games with unfailing originality, has told me of something which to him seemed a sign of that beauty. It was a slight incident to witness, and harder for me to select in words than for him: a child's ball flung into the "battlefield"; an illustrious cricketer fielding there; his gathering the ball at the first opportunity, his smiling grace as he went over to restore it. A princely gesture he made of it—one of the princes of cricket, and of India.

XIX

Beyond the Ground

HERE just beneath the crown of the hill, overlooking a shallow moorish valley which opens out of the highland, I lie in the most unabashed posture of indolence. Never did high summer connive more genially at such a lazy mood; and besides in days like these of austerity I have not been merely wheeled to this scene, past which behind a high hedge a big road goes, but it takes no notice of my valley nor the valley of it. The long walk was sunny and strenuous, and most of the way it skirted hawthorn arbours where one wise old cow and another stood sleepily, tugging leaves in the shade. I passed the farm on the creek of the willowed river, the crossing of the tracks on which the farmer's boy in his blue shirt and tumbled felt hat was going cheerfully with his two dogs, the silent woods where the nightingales were singing not long ago, the tall stone house and garden wall behind which the Rambler himself, our unescapable Samuel Johnson, LL.D., was known to fall into praise of a country life. The counterpane of the great champaign country, tinted between its dividing lines of hedge with the harvest yellows and greys, began to spread out in full view as I traced the ridge road under the elms. There should have been thunder by all the signs, but a breeze had come in just enough strength to change the feeling, and to thin the haze which even so wrapped all this world in a soft dim bloom. Then at the point where you could almost hear the coach of the long ago mounting the rise, where still the remnant trunk of an elm seen by the hot-faced passengers in its full branchery was able to clothe itself in green, I found my gate (well pegged with the iron pin of untold age) and I captured solitude at a step.

Here then I stretch my legs, I recline on a tapestry of short grass and clover and fernweed and small yellow flowers calling for the designer's notice and some starry white ones to which the lambstoe is a giant. The bramble bush behind me screens me more or less from the sun, but I do not want the humid shade to-day—I ask the radiance in the open to do its work with my skin and bone. Down there is the moorish valley, figured with other clumpy brambles like queer animals grazing, and a large fringe of bracken, and lanky ragwort tinselling the picture as if it were a fair. Nobody wants the place, to-day at least, and I am not going a yard farther; but my idleness is not a coma. I at least keep my senses open to the transactions of the small tenants here, who have a rather awesome grove to hide in over on the far side of the hollow; its oak, tower to the ridge, gloomy and still, and out of their swarthy green starts up one tall dead white tree, its long fingers outspread in a manner of monitory signal. It is a relief to perceive through the spaces between the high domes of the oakwood good innocent wheatfield, ripe-tanned, triumphant on the open acres.

Never was there a poorer naturalist than I, but I have loved Nature and am able to be as pleased with her characteristic looks and preoccupations and voices as with those (almost) of my true love. Here I stay, as an Elizabethan courtier-poet is always telling us he would, "content with hip, and haw and bramble-berry"; and here the worst naturalist may constantly know of something going on. Bee, fly, butterfly are ever passing me here, or flitting and zigzagging out among those golden-blossomed weeds. An elegant figure, neither bee nor wasp, long and slender and black and white, hovers with intense poise at the flower by my hand. I did not expect to see green woodpeckers hopping about among the thrushes and blackbirds among the ant-hills, but I may watch them now, it seems, as long as I will. They and the ragwort, at this distance, are of the same colour. They are never long away from home, and the yaffling in the oakwood is probably domestic talk of the correctest kind—their cries are about as melodious as a penny whistle. With loud clappings of wings the pigeons suddenly launch forth from the verdurous summits, glide and circle a time or two, and roost afresh; roo-coo, roo-coo, the wood resounds. And by myself on a hillock beside the cattle-track above the beds of fern, a magpie dances about, a son of mischief, but perhaps not man's mischief. Through all I hear the chatter of the smaller birds, and the murmur of an insect multitude invisible, and when a plane passes over this upland it merely increases the desultory but not indifferent tones of so primitive a place.

I ask myself, when have I been more fortunate in recreation? why should I go from here, or seek elsewhere for diversion? how could I have yielded so many hours to any other kinds of play but this? The only sporting events here are the chases of butterflies, who do not seem to care who wins in the end, or that magpie stepping eyefully round a stone—but he is more likely performing some conjuration than perfecting his footwork. Yes, this is a way to pass the time which I shall not forget, and "I have been here before." But while I examine my inner self a little more closely I discern that this preference and this contentment among the yellow linnets and purple thistles are not so hard, so long as a world war keeps life among men thin and shorn of its usual allurements. In other years, such is the condition of humanity, I might have failed to reach this hill and valley, such features as the cricket pavilion intervening. And would it not have been about now that . . .

It is a little confusing, but I think that I recognise this place, and that grand stand. What is this paper I am so tightly grasping? Why, of course, a Rover's Ticket; indeed without this magic paper I should not have been seated here right against the ropes, with such a perfect view of the turf and the wicket only waiting for the action. That hand-bell sounds like it should; and those white coats come solemnly forth into the sun according to the laws of Nature. And who is that, soon afterwards emerging? the Majesty of

Gloucestershire! It is W. R. Hammond, and the others of the like intention are after him—one of them is telling some gorgeous story as they go; I hope E. Hendren will field over here, for he will probably tell the story to us as well if ever the Australians lose a wicket, or a pause for lemonade is permitted. And is Leyland's shoulder really better?

But why does not the game really begin? In some apprehension I turn to my neighbour, who happens to be and surely must be no other than Charles Marriott, but he is curiously unconcerned. He is behaving very strangely in fact. He has defined the known conventions of Test Match spectatorship by bringing a butterfly net with him and chasing a wasp with it. I see. . . . There is the little valley of the woodpeckers with the outcast bushes and the yellow-headed weeds, and I am awake and the time is come for my homeward walk. It is a little saddening to find that the great match even in a dream never got beyond the point at which the batsmen were just due. By now the delay in that detail has lasted some years, but if we may pay any attention to the dreaming mind it is no more than an interruption. They will come at last, and the contented multitude seeing them come will scarcely remember that there ever was any delay, or doubt, or rumour of abandonment.

The homeward walk itself would be recreation divinely good, I know, to a great number of our Englishmen and Englishwomen who are at this hour serving their country in far different scenes. This tiny village of grey walls and deep-set windows and thatched roofs and more roses, nasturtiums and lavender than even Helen Allingham used to crowd into a picture, feels and tells of their absence. It is little changed, if changed at all, from the village they left, not knowing when they would return; a load of bombs which tumbled absurdly from the cloud of night and gouged out mighty craters in one of the near meadows is ancient history, and the craters have disappeared. An elderly woman sits watching, as if someone would be coming into sight round the churchyard wall, at her front door; two little girls with brilliant hair, which they have been treating very thoughtfully, promenade past the village hall as if to keep up the style of the older enchantresses far away now in uniform or factory kit. A "mongrel grim" wanders forth opposite the inn in all the show of anger at my intrusive steps, but he merely wants someone to talk to. His friends are nearly all away. Probably the man who is getting out his bicycle next door is in the same situation; he looks of the age to have been away himself last war, and I guess from his type, his build and face and movement that he will keep the new generation in touch with their cricket and football, and duly collect their subscriptions, when they in their turn come back.

The village and its orchards are now hidden from me, the path through the wheatfield has brought me into the next wide valley, and into the shadows of a fine row of high elms. Down in the dip the dormer windows of an ancient farm house peer over the barn roofs and the crooked apple trees at the bounteous harvest, the hayfields, the blue-veiled hills. I survey the many-coloured, hedge-cantoned, gentle-contoured miles of good land, and find in my heart the verses which Milton in his holidaying youth wrote for deathless love of such places:

> Some time walking not unseen
> By hedge-row elms, on hillocks green,
> Right against the eastern gate,
> Where the great Sun begins his state,
> Rob'd in flames and amber light,
> The clouds in thousand liveries dight,
> While the ploughman near at hand
> Whistles o'er the furrow'd land,
> And the milk-maid singeth blith,
> And the mower whets his sithe. . . .

But then, this valley is as likely as any other to have been the element whence Milton formed his vision of a delightful landscape. Ahead of me rises the still wooded hill of Shotover where his grandfather was underranger of the forest; and there too is Forest Hill, which at one time must have seemed to the poet the most beautiful ascent in all the world. One Whitsuntide, his nephew says with a wink across three centuries, "he took a journey into the country; nobody about him certainly knowing the reason, or that it was more than a journey of recreation; after a month's stay, home he returns a married man that went out a bachelor; his wife being Mary, the eldest daughter of Mr. Richard Powell, then a justice of peace of Foresthil, near Shotover, in Oxfordshire." And so . . .

> Meadows trim with daisies pied,
> Shallow brooks, and rivers wide,

and all the rest of that flowing song of scenery. But here I am at one of the shallow brooks, and the children are there before me dancing time away; I do not think I will hurry unduly to come out on the flaring by-pass road.

XX

The Road Runs On

AFTER ALL, "a journey of recreation," though it be but of a few miles or a few hours, is the pastime that can be taken by all ages and under more conditions than the rest. I was more than once invited by the wise in the very battlefield when there was nothing urgent to expect or to do, to "come for a walk," and gladly did so; the country was we may say a little disordered, the orchards were full of ammunition dumps and waterlogged dugouts, the shrine at the chateau corner had lost its door and its saint had lost most of his plaster, the chateau was a skeleton among the half-burnt fir-trees; and yet our spirits rose, we were going for a walk. The fly in a black silk coat with red decorations, settling on the sunflower leaf in the wild garden by the church wall, more gap than wall, was our emblem for the moment; he basked, he quested, and off he flew without respect to war-gods.

And they were not satisfied. I should have thought that they might have been when our route no longer showed a bough or any other green thing.—During this new war, I have felt like one of the willows by the terrible Yser Canal, which stood unwrenched, unannihilated, though the iron pierced deep into it, while the surrounding world was in a furnace. I have been capriciously spared, and yet the burden has been upon me possibly more because the Anno Domini question, on which I used to hear our Vicar laughingly and yet seriously comment on a Sunday morning, has left me in a corner. *Suave mari magno*; happy feels the man who is in a secure post of observation whence he can watch at all points of the compass all the others in difficulty. So the ancient poet tried to persuade us; he was human, and I have felt something of this human suavity; but I must always be in some sort out with the others who are not in my coign of vantage. It is still as true as Lucretius when the other Roman writes *Homo sum : nihil humanum a me alienum puto.* When young, I did not perceive how great a disaster a great war brought to the sympathies and lifelong yearnings of older people; but I am no longer young.

Therefore I have sought relief, and what can be finer relief, more vital recreation than the land we live in? It has not been sufficiently praised, even to this day. Its lovely and unfading blessings are not all in the Blue Guide; nor do they require of us a costly and laborious business in order that we may receive them. A journey of recreation is simple, and the horses need not be saddled nor the petrol regulations defied. We shall walk it, and it will be our fault if we do not win the match.

The country churches of England alone would supply a man from youth to age with a recreation in the richest meaning of the word, were there no others. With no knowledge of the history of religion, of art and architecture, of heraldry, of social change and the mutability of ambitions—with no technical terms of nicety for the details from vane to vault, and east window to west door—even so we may play the beautiful and heart-easing game of village churches, or town churches either, but the other is the more varied and adventurous. It has as much of sheer discovery in it as a voyage to where you will; for the million yesterdays have become quite as strange to to-day as distance round the world and its contrasts can be. Think, for instance, of an ordinary modern epitaph, and think of this incomplete one which I noted as we leaned against the sunny grassbank in sight of a huge tower with stone coffins of a much older day (the mind ceased to try to reach it) propped about its base:

Know Posterity that on the 8th of April in the year of grace 1757 the rambling remains of the abovesaid John Dale were in the 86th year of his pilgrimage laid upon his two wives.

This thing in life might raise some jealousie:
here all three lye together lovingly;
But from embraces here no pleasure flows,
alike are here all human joys and woes.
Here Sarah's chiding John no longer hears
and old John's rambling Sarah no more
     fears.
A period's come to all their toilsome lives,
the goodman's quiet, still are both his wives.

Turn from this again to one of the great tombs which so
many of our hardly visited churches yet contain, and the
recumbent effigies of lord and lady in their sumptuous
raiment, with their hounds big and little at their feet, their
proud hands praying, their faces fixed upon the coming
Judgment; and how vast and fantastic our English scene
becomes. Would we still fathom it in another bank and
shoal of time? These wall tablets of geometrical white
polished marble, still so little touched with age though from
the times of Nelson and Canning, at once deepen the magic
of the storied past; how far away they are from what we
pondered on just now, and what we feel at this present
stroke of time, though *that* is beaten by the clock up above
in the gloom somewhere with the same careful and solemn
syllable as was known to these dead of the Regency. Their
characters are here defined, the priest's, the justice's, the
young mother's, the statesman's, the tradesman's, in elabo-
rate appreciation and prose. We are reminded of the *Man
of Feeling* and *The Sorrows of Werther*. We could not see our
own contemporaries in these ways, nor express them in
these moral and sentimental epithets. The veil that flows
upon that exquisite urn there at the head of the In Memo-
riam is of a weaving now impossible, but it was once not
only possible but universal. . . . "Reader! If a disposition
courteous and amiable amid fortunes unpropitious and
obscure may move the heart, if a union of accomplishments
never flaunted and learning never suffered to intervene

between the possessor and the duties of quotidian sympathy may claim. . . ."

First catch your hare—the advice is sound; and first find your church—but that is not hard; this everywhere is our happy island inheritance. When we come upon it, its offerings are many, and each church has its own; hence all the experts, all the "transactions." The rest of us may happen with delight on the miscellany of any church—it may have a stone cross there by the yew tree, its old gravestones may have cherubims still looking large-eyed on the grasses, with a tint of red on the lips and gold on the plumes after all these years. The sun plays yet on the scratch-dial without a peg which the labourer consulted in the days before Henry VIII. and that gold-handed tower clock which strikes on such a vibrant bell. Those monster heads at the top corners of the tower are sculptures which make our modern exhibitions look a little deficient in the department of grotesque; they grin down from the blue sky upon the graves and primroses and the girl who sits on the table tomb in the radiance of her springtime. Within the church, its personality, which no word can catch for a second; yet one may take in some characteristics—discern the hatchments and enjoy the special rampant humours of the Lion and Unicorn about the Royal arms, or the calligraphy of the local man so long ago who has inscribed in good gold letters on pitch-black panels the benefactions that are now so homely, the annual £1 for cakes for the cottage children, or £5 for a schoolmaster for them; one may pore upon the fragments of flower-coloured glass, legend and landscape, or delicately outlined and piercingly individual portrait, where the light comes cool through the deep rift in the wall. There are churches yet where the dark oak pews, and chests, and tables, and pulpit are all in their old order, and you may fancy yourself the naughty undevout boy in the squire's box, lurking out of the line of vision of parson and clerk. Or you may glow with the pride of the wood-carver as he completed the blossoms and sprigs of his taste in these panels, and though he could not quite find room for the text the church-wardens gave him yet provided enough (with an &c.) for the searcher of the scriptures to recognise. Here within also the mediæval sculptor has left us, close to the great black beams of the roof, his own little gallery, daring stone faces ideal and faces mischievous, heavenly beauty in a maiden or original sin in a musician; or as we stoop round the font we find graphic yet riddling narrative of the Christian mystery, and our English world is enlarged to our freshened imaginative sympathies in a moment beyond all our measures. Coming nearer our own tenancy of time a little, we dream over the Victorian piety which shines in the embroideries and the shining brass and lily-vases and offertory dishes at the altar; we try to define that piety, those communicants, their approach to the deity whom they believed to be so conscious of their own kneel-ings and prayings and observances, all ultimately empurpled in the expanses of stained glass memorials—the richest that ever were made by conspiring science, and art, and progress, and investments—to which it is not unlikely that some older and humbler form of art was meekly sacrificed. But all the contraries are at home here. An old church is like a big family, at a perpetual reunion; and its fascination comes largely from its eccentricities of detail and its harmonising central spirit.

And I watch Cordelia the booklover, turning over the redolent covers and pages of the Hymns, the Prayers, the Church Services, the Forms for occasions, the Testaments. How gloryingly they came in here with their fresh inscrip-tions of ownership—and how surprisingly they have grown old! From 1843 to—just now has passed so quickly;—they are still in their appointed places, but no one ever thought of their first owners for many a year. In a really gloomy corner of a gloomy pew, beneath a misplaced hassock, Cordelia dislodges a very large volume in driest leather covers—no other than a copy of the Authorised Version of A.D. 1611. It has rested there apparently for some years, but it seems to say that it wishes for nothing else. It is a foundation, and as such it can remain without distress in the background. But from its red and black pages, as Cordelia brings them into the church-light, its noble typography grandly declares the glory of God and the certainty of the wonders of his work in the making of the world and establishing of his temple. So seen, the Authority becomes a hundred times clearer to our senses, and the Church, we feel afresh, will be changeless; changeless to me, too, my Cordelia in such places, her brightness and her melody there, her quietness and her meditation.

Thinking of all the silent Past about us, we sit a little longer in the Church porch, and a warm breeze is springing up and there is a great sighing in the leaves outside; the sky darkens, the lightning flash silvers the white walls for an instant, the storm speaks. From the river valley as the shower begins like water-smoke and the wind gushes forth from the crags, the threshing of the trees sends its own swelling hymn; and when we set forth again the world is sparkling with sun and raindrop, so that we would be for ever on the road, if the flowers leave room for a road.

That road, now a highway and now a meadow path, has led us to so many treasures in its time; now it brought the spacious prospect over half the county, now some enclosed little hiding place of wild flowers by a tiny rill; we did well to trust ourselves to it for our pastime. One day it slid round the old clay walls and unkempt yards of a declining village with houses of a dignity that told of other times, and it crossed the footbridges, and left us by the green pools of the idlest of rivers, where under the willows you played your part in an unprepared scene of Leda and the Swan. And another day, it lured us back to the same place—do you remember?—but the floods of November were fast rising over the pastures, and in the wild flashes of sunset the cattle on the peninsula of dry ground were looking worried; nobody came. Then you cleverly persuaded them to move from the midst of the swirling waters, and over the bridge into the safer grounds where later the forgetful farmer's boy would find them—a simple happiness, but of such memories life is made. Shall we forget, far along our mazy road which runs through all the seasons, the high-backed bridge on the Aldershot canal on that winter afternoon, dead still with frost, when the woods were gilded curtains of flame-like silks? or that snow-like moonlight and mist over the lake when the echo from the far shore repeated your Latin verses and your name and the names of some who were far away? Through the copses ran the road, a mossy path now, where the wood-spurge smiled at us for fancying that it was rare; and once or twice we were held in a sudden silence by the tragic touch that even the most smiling mood of Nature cannot avoid—the calf dead and all but swallowed up in the clay slough at the field corner, the wether's still swollen body a little apart from the feeding flock. But ever the road went on to give us a world apart from serious and cramped routines, and now its borders were mighty hillsides, and soaring towers of limestone, and forests of light-green ash, and ferny wildernesses; and in the blaze of a conquering sun, the "humble flower" the rag-wort was seen in gorgeous array as golden-blazing as he, here massing in tall bushy-helmed battalions on the steep greensward, there tasselling the pinnacle with a single merry torch of blossom. And still the playing waters sang below.

In solitudes like those we have had triumphs which to us seemed finer than any in other recreations; some may be familiar with them daily, but there is much in the unfamiliar. We must treasure our winnings. As we passed the great warren on the side of the moor, there was a scuffle, and two or three rabbits came hastening out, one of them a king of rabbits. We quickly saw why. A fine weasel was already in retreat; he had been prowling in hope of finding a victim or two; and now, while the king made as if he would pursue him with vengeance, his lean brown shape was running away with all speed. This was hardly what we had expected. But presently we were again allowed to win something from "Nature's infinite book of secrecy." Two crows were strutting on the hill, and a very knowing dog came bounding and threatening towards them. They let him come to the point at which he might almost have seized them, then all of a sudden they quite vanished, leaving dog and spectators puzzled. It must have been an old trick of theirs. They had, at their own time, just gone to earth in the empty rabbit-burrows there. Witnessing these things, we wondered much for all our love of human beings and their sports and games if there could be anything better than wandering as Richard Jefferies did, and the joys of the naturalist became singularly attractive. It is Life that is the greatest of all the pastimes, and to discover something of it is a big enough score; we may all be champions here, for chance is great in this matter. The leaf-cutter bee came and worked in the hedge of a little town garden, day after day, without any arrangement of ours, and we were as lucky then as any entomologist in England. We chanced to look over into the neglected backwater close to the cinema with the buses by, and we were the only people in all likelihood who that spring saw what was in progress there: the water-play, the nuptial tourneyings of a pair of mating grayling. Ever as our byway proceeds I feel a deeper understanding of every student of Nature, and have begun to wish I had even been a speleologist and wormed my way into the pot-holes as these most skilful and valiant escapers do.

There are some whose sport is house-hunting—not for the actual end of occupying the houses they discover, but for the reward of beauty, fantasy, guessing. The tiniest cabin, the lordliest hall may be equal in their regard, so long as it has a certain ghost-story to tell, not necessarily a painful or a horrid one, nor of the past alone; for the sun-shine has its phantom world, and the future can come this way in dream children. It fascinates me simply to study the looks of those who are natural geniuses at this pastime of occupying in fancy a myriad homes, a variety of periods up

and down this land. Of course I may not always interpret
their countenances accurately; and while I watch "the rapt
soul sitting in those eyes" and feel that the vision of peri-
wigged ancestry or carefree posterity is in progress, it may
be that the real thought runs on what should be done if we
had the place with that overgrown thicket of rhododen-
drons, or the huge stables and idle pigeon-house, or maybe
the question of hot water system or telephone. And could
we live where there is not a river or a brook within sight
and hearing? We might try this

> Cottage near a wood
> Where larks and thrushes sing,

and rescue the remains of an orchard from present distress,
and have a bright little pony and trap—but perhaps a car.
. . . Would it be too expensive to keep up all that garden,
without which the charm might vanish—the ghosts might
flee away? There would be a brewing-house, and a vast
cellar, and tremendous cupboards, and a view of the glittering hills and a blue sea between them, and a study big
enough for all the books, and such a nursery with just acres
of room for their games. . . .

There are some whose sport is bookshop-hunting in the
market towns. It makes an itinerary of wonderful hopes and
perhaps almost equal disappointments, but somewhere the
triumph will be waiting. Somewhere the unexamined hoard
of rare and blessed literature . . .

Well, it is all Cordelia's road.

XXI

Wednesday's Match

BUT all this (scanty as it is in comparison with our road) seems to have taken me, in the words of the poet Wilde, "far from the cricket ground and noisy eight." It may not have done so, or else the road returns with its travellers at a thought; for I am not deceived in thinking that this bordering on it is the cricket ground and that the stumps are standing there in the brightness for the Wednesday match of which I think I made a mention. The practice nets are up, and the sweatered form of the Colonel is seen there in majestic loneliness, as he bowls a perfect length with a prehistoric ball at an invisible batsman. He very soon has me in there, not that it makes much difference—but now the opponent Captain is arriving, and he is a youth of great sweetness. No one, least of all the Colonel, would rebuff him for admitting at the start that his side is one of twelve men, not the regulation eleven. Of course, let them all come! The Colonel's mysterious team is to play one of R.A.F. cadets, and the suspicion is that eleven of them will be far too many for us; "but, however." The R.A.F. cadet Captain is known to me; he brought me his essay on "The Duchess of Malfi" only a day or two ago, so perhaps he will get his own back in a moment.

We bat. The Colonel's half-crown is usually obedient, I guess. The Colonel's eye has been on me, and he is coming to a decision: I am to go in, with another player who from long experience of cricketers in pavilions is not so worried as I am at this priority. But I am not only alarmed; I regret that my attention is inclined to stray. It is taken by the summer picture all round this green square, by those stone walls and those warm brick ones, by the scarlet runners and onion-heads which crowd one corner, by the hollyhocks and dahlias and roses which orb the setting with their pretty colours; and I wish I might be sauntering round in freedom to take a real look at the apple trees and the copper beech and the Lombardy poplars. Even the neo-Gothic architecture accuses me of having put off and put off the real pastime which it has prepared for us. Something like this will happen to me on the Day of Judgment—and I shall not be the only one.

Off we go. The fast bowler (from Canterbury) is built for his job, and the boys run, pick up and throw in as if the future of the Royal Air Force depended on every one of these actions. The planes over us do not distract them from this immediate ground evolution. The light is sharply white, and I wonder what it is like in Sicily where the guns are the fast bowlers. Still, the human type who is banging away at me is my proper subject. My partner in the blue cap at first took his business a little casually, but he does so no longer; and we settle down to a kind of siege warfare. I find it roasting work at that; and gaze away on any intermission at the coloured gardens, and the coloured dresses in the chairs outside the pavilion, and the low battlemented church tower with its louvred window, mouthing gargoyle and Picardy-recalling turret. But we have still to make something of the innings. At least we are making it last out in point of time; and when we are on our way to the pavilion, something is felt to have been achieved—the heat and our stolidity have tired that fine young pace bowler.

It might not signify greatly to the Colonel and his partner who are now at the wicket if this strategic exhaustion had not been brought about. The Colonel, a Free Forester, has played so many an innings with a complete fluency that he hardly notices anything except the supply of balls for him to drive and sweep and cut. His partner, who has also had lots of experience, has a curious faculty of perceiving beforehand what the bowler will do, and knowing what he does in this psychic way he can bring off the most flashing shots exactly where there is no body to obstruct them. It looks to me like genius, I hear that he has treated bowlers of the first rank to the same graceful but bewildering punishment which the poor cadets, no matter which one it is sending the ball up, are now getting. The tins on the scoreboard do their best to keep in touch with the mounting total, the boys go on fielding in a style which makes me fancy they are all Australians—and now the Colonel with his gallant half-century of runs and his fellow-smiter with somewhere towards a hundred are coming in, followed by the not ungrateful fieldsmen. The innings is declared closed, and the tea-table declared open.

But the Colonel is not to be lightly deflected from his purpose, and time is short for its fulfilment. I have to leave a whole pint of R.A.F. tea, or somewhere near that, unenjoyed. I was trying to skulk with it and admire a picture of the blue sea and a brave ship—I was detected, and ordered to put on my wicket-keeping equipment. A faint appeal for mercy on account of old age is met by the Colonel with an unanswerable reference to his own chronology. Enter the opening batsmen, tall lads with powerful arms, and I should have forecast that they would go comfortably along until the time for drawing stumps; but cricket is still a queer game. Our bowling strength is uncertain even to the Colonel with his preparatory "exhaustive inquiries," and at one end the performer serves up more desperate no-balls and wides than practicable ones. At the other we have a left-handed man, with a modest manner and an agricultural speech, whose pace is evidently quite lively and whose run comes rapidly round from behind the umpire. I wonder . . . Yes. He gets going. His pace grows, he gets the ball to move back from the leg stump to the middle, he accents one now and then with small sign of it in his action. Probably he does not have to think this out in words—he too has that lucky gift, cricket genius. The boys are up against it. Even their own geniuses, whom I have seen in most dangerous displays, are not able to feel settled though they evade trouble for a while. Meanwhile a change of bowling at the other end reminds me, if I need to be reminded, that out of cricket there comes always some new thing. The new bowler is very tall, and he takes about three slow steps to the crease, whereupon he bowls a ball of extreme violence. The speed varies; there must be some way of knowing; and —well, that one nearly knocked me off my feet. The next bounced to the top of my jump and stretch.

With these phenomena coming into action against them, the cadets have a poor time of it and I watch them meeting their problem with a cheerful realisation. The evening approaches, and the cadence of the game seems to go with the creeping shadows. The voices of church and college clocks come and go, the spectators on the wall are drifting away; and there are not many moments left for play, but these we find are likely to be too many for the last of the batting side to survive. But let no man utter, though his breast harbour, such a sentiment! There is no telling. This time, however, our left-hander is quite remorseless, down swings his fastest one, the bail leaps into the hands of first slip, and the match is all over. But what was the Colonel saying to me at the nets, which perhaps is not likely to be forgotten as soon as this one game?

It was on the future of cricket, and how to save the game from the death which he had heard a great player predict for it, or even ascribe to it already: Cricket is dead. The Colonel had plans for its resuscitation, and among them naturally another Wednesday match at the first opportunity, but he aired some broader and more remarkable plans too; they may be needed. I shall not let these pavilion cats out of his bag, and am not yet reduced to the vision of this game's corpse; the sad event has been brooded over before, and engaged gravest intellects a long time ago. Anthony Trollope in the sixties, editing a volume on *British Sports and Pastimes*, was not very hopeful in his diagnosis of the state of the game. He did not think that it was in a worse way than the others, but his knowledge of it brought it within the "very serious question . . . whether it may not be the case that we are overdoing our Sport, and making it too grand in its outlines, and too important in its details." I do not know now the next of his comments which I shall quote would have been received down in Barsetshire: "There is an old saying that whatever you do, you should do well —which like many other old sayings is very untrue, and very dangerous in its lack of truth. But nowhere is this more untrue than in reference to our amusements." And regretting the usurpation of his times by the immorality behind this awful motto he comes to cricket: "Even Cricket has become such a business, that there arises a doubt in the minds of amateur players whether they can continue the sport. . . . The danger which we have indicated is the rock against which our Sports may possibly be made shipwreck."

Perhaps Trollope, like the modern cricketer whose Ichabod the Colonel was quoting to me as he straightened up the stumps, was going a little too far. One of his contributors ventured to discriminate between the temperature of Cricket and the other patients: "The necessity for training has not yet forced itself very strongly upon the cricketing mind. A man who could exceed in beer the day before a University boat-race would certainly be capable of murdering his aunt; whereas a cricketer guilty of a parallel excess would probably shrink, we may say from any injury to the same relative of a deeper dye than assault and battery." Indeed, there is not even in the records section of Wisden's *Cricketer's Almanack* any instance of a cricketer laying a bat on the person of his aunt.

Since Trollope was a fox-hunting man the conditions which might send cricket to earth for ever have changed a little; and the principal disadvantage of which he did not know is the passion that the little boys now have for the air. It is in vain that I produce bat and ball to one or two known to me. I might as well ask them to sit down and play a game of Goose; indeed, since that implies an endless round of drinks, and they are clever boys, they might agree to that. Meanwhile, their talk is of—Lancasters, Mitchells, Fortresses, Ju's (if I heard correctly); and they sit on sunny days even zealously building and painting models of such wonderful machines, as though the question of a little diversion with the splintered Crawford's Exceller and the compo ball so essential to the boys who flourished once did not arise.

To continue with the characteristics of the day which seem to portend the extinction of cricket might lead me into a mood of despondency almost amounting to agreement with the Colonel's friend. I hear elegies on the breeze:

> Calm is the morn without a sound,
>   Except the local Plane Club's drone,
>   And one black crow that croaks alone
> On what was once the cricket ground.
>
> Calm in the moss'd pavilion all,
>   Save where the rats are trying on
>   The umpires' coats, or gaunt grey don
> Hopes to dig up a "cricket ball."
>
> Up in the Press Box nothing stirs,
>   Except the amorous Spider who
>   Devours her mate to prove him true;
> The only score to-day is hers. . . .

Away with such nocturnes for future Bank Holidays; we shall all be there as usual, parson and people, and even the little boys will be asking which player is Fishlock and who it was who caught Pope (A.) out. And at the interval there will be the customary assembly round the roped-off pitch, staring at it with dumb and infinite respect (at least, I think mostly we have to leave it at that)—the very grass, the "little patch of ground," on which the boot-studs of the heroes were in action hardly a moment ago.

XXII

On a Trait of English Poetry

" A GRACE without a name." After all the attempts that
I have made in my time to find the central and unique
reason for the captivating ways of cricket, and to set down
in words the magic principle, I am back at the beginning.
Perhaps this is the dilemma, or the escape, of all our critical
appreciations in all the regions of the delightful, beautiful
and attractive. Let Aristotle, or Ruskin, or Roger Fry, or
C. B. Fry himself do what they will, there still remains the
unknown quantity or the "unpurchaseable light" within
the work of art discussed and explained—just the last little
thing, but without it what would be worth discussing? It
may not be the same thing that makes genius and loveliness
what they are throughout existence, but only these words
appear to suit it in its variety, "a grace without a name."
For this reason perhaps we should be most grateful to those
whose habit it is to express the charm of what they love less
in a direct designation than in an impression, or gracious
response created from their own feelings. We do not possess
the literal or pictorial evidence of the beauty of Mr. W. H.
We have the radiance of it in the verse of Shakespeare upon
his own state of mind within its domination. We have a
portrait of Joseph Munden, comedian (who died in 1832),
in one of his parts. How minor a thing even this honest
and accurate document is in comparison with the vision
of Charles Lamb as he enjoyed Munden's acting: "He was
imaginative; he could impress upon an audience an *idea*—
the low one perhaps of a leg of mutton and turnips; but
such was the grandeur and singleness of his expressions,
that such single expression would convey to all his auditory
a notion of all the pleasures they had all received from all

the legs of mutton *and turnips* they had ever eaten in all their lives. Now this is not *acting*, nor do I set down Munden amongst my old actors. He was only a wonderful man, exerting his vivid impressions through the agency of the stage."

If my impression that English poetry has not found a great deal to say directly on cricket and other games and sports of ours is not far wrong, I have also felt that one element in it has always been a quality of enjoyment akin to that which is the best in them. It is "a grace without a name," but perhaps I may endeavour by one or two trials of terms, and better by a few particular instances, to come a little nearer to locating it. I mean the kind of poems which, however else we may ascribe them to one class or another, really exercise their fascination over us by reason of some eternal youthfulness and spirit of "life itself a playing holiday" in the minds whence they arose. The anthologist might collect them into various camps according to their forms and subjects, but their delightfulness would remain the same through them all, refusing subdivisions.

This French anthology by me here is entitled *Chansons Libres et Joyeuses*, and yet its poems are of another sort than our own free and joyous compositions. They are mostly on the prospects, pranks, successes and dilemmas of the hotly amorous. We might assemble our own volumes of these; but the liberty and merry-making of our poetry do not greatly belong to those gardens of gallantry.

> What more felicity can fall to creature
> Than to enjoy delight with liberty?

The sense of these lines is large and like the cloudless sky, to which indeed they belong in their place—that sweet dream of Spenser's *The Fate of the Butterfly*. Even death and death's antique rites may under the sunshine of our poet's happy and transcending grace become a part of their fairy world. Ages ago the exquisite spirit of Skelton, who could be a scourge where he saw the need, was moved to console a little girl on the death of her sparrow Philip in a lyrical parallel of the great burial service—a paradise of birds rather, an "appropriate country" where the child might wander past her tears into the enchanted woods of life unassailable. Later that mysterious man Shakespeare, desired to write an elegy on a loving couple, did something in the same way, and treating the occasion as a fable already, the "obsequy" of the Phœnix and the Turtle, arranged a stately ritual in his verse wherein all the good birds had their place; but he, moreover, was pleased to mingle with this imaginative diversion the holiday of the metaphysician, and to throw off with the ease of a fiddler playing his dozens of tunes at a wake the most beautiful of intellectual subtleties in purest form of statement.

> Love hath reason, reason none,
> If what parts can so remain.

It is not to be passed over that the first great book in poetic attire which we inherit is a holiday book. The *Canterbury Tales* of Chaucer might so easily have been so different a contribution. There in his view as a subject was the pilgrimage of those who set out

> The holy blissful Martyr for to seek
> That them had holpen when that they were sick.

One can imagine how this purpose, with the image and solemn glory of Thomas à Becket's shrine overtowering the lives of the pious, might have drawn from a poet a number of saintly odes, confessions, litanies and petitions of severe and cloistered unity. This is not what we have, and though Chaucer himself at the end of his days was afraid that it is what we ought to have had from him, some refer that recantation not so much to his mind in its strength as to his last illness and the persuasions of the priests attending him out of the bright world into a mystery. But no doubt the Wife of Bath has long since consented to overlook this obscure episode; and we continue in possession of a pilgrimage rather to the spiritual home of Harry Bailly the Landlord, of ease of mind rather than to the hair shirts and step hollowed by innumerable kneelings.

So far, this is poetry openly choosing the merrier and gayer side of things; but Chaucer has other works in which the golden drop of humorous beauty is instilled almost without his own attention. The wonders of his House of Fame, or Parliament of Fowls, are gathered by him like cowslips and daisies by children in a spring meadow. The second of these poems, we are told by his editor, is in fact an allegorical celebration of the wooing by King Richard II. of the Lady Anne of Bohemia, and King Richard is duly honoured as the "formel egle," the noblest of Nature's works; but this does not dictate to the poet's pleasant spirit any timid formality as a whole. The birds quite forget, in the party that they hold, the high occasion which is their cue, and gossip away about their families as though a king's wedding were all in the day's work. The eloquence of the goose, the rustic candour of the duck, the disdain of the merlin for the cuckoo come merrily over the affairs of monarchs, and when at last the birds choose a few of their number to sing a round we are in a world without a care or a doubt:

> Now welcome summer, with thy sunnë softe,
> That hast this winter's weather overshake
> And driven away the longë nightës blacke.
> Saint Valentine, that art full high alofte,
> Thus singen smallë fowlës for thy sake,
> Now welcome summer, with thy sunnë softe
> That hast this winter's weather overshake,
> And driven away the longë nightës blacke. . . .

This is in truth the poetry of diversion. Ancient or

modern, our men of genius spontaneously break into it. "Monstrous Milton" was not to be confined all his days to the theological and the political themes which have yielded through him the sublimest parts of English verse. We know him just as much in the straying "unimportance" of his two poems singing of cheerfulness and seriousness, poems which perhaps he never meant to keep in contradistinction all along, for both are poems of delight. *L'Allegro* and *Il Penseroso* are inseparable friends in the landscape of leisure and dream. Both poems outwit the material world, send the wars and the debates and the statute-books to bed, and then—

> Young and old come forth to play
> On a Sunshine Holy day.

There is no grief in the shadows here; there are old legends, the story of Orpheus among them, but it is the beauty of his song and the reward of his love which Milton revives. The storm at daybreak which the melancholy spirit desires is a musical one and closes with a pretty run of quiet little notes:

> Thus night oft see me in thy pale career,
> Till civil-suited Morn appeer,
> Not trickt and frounc't as she was wont,
> With the Attick Boy to hunt,
> But Cherchef't in a comly Cloud,
> While rocking Winds are Piping loud,
> Or usher'd with a shower still,
> When the gust hath blown his fill,
> Ending on the russling leaves,
> With minute drops from off the Eaves.

To my taste, this is the voice of a subtle humour, and the world thus perceived is not one of which we can grow weary. Milton could write what is usually called for as comic and joking verse, witness his punning lines on Hobson the Carrier; but his lyrical truant-playing is incomparably finer, "higher far descended."

Somewhere in his letters Percy Bysshe Shelley, with a smile in the writing, says that he is making a joke, but that nobody ever allows him the quality of making a joke. This attitude towards him has remained, and the extraordinary flights and spiritual voyages of his poetry are quite sufficient to explain it. He, if any one, appears to outsoar our general experience and the manners of our emotions. He has been labelled an angel, with subsidiary docketing, so often that he must almost believe it himself by now. But he did not in his day, and it has been my contention that his poems must sometimes be regarded without angelical prejudice. They include some of the most perfect examples of the English way of being "not wholly serious," yet signifying the triumph of life. What a pastime the existence of *The Cloud* is as he imagines and sings it! Can a cloud laugh, even though gods and spirits riding on it may? Shelley, living through the freaks and masquings and magical mischief of his glorious Cloud—did any poet before him play at being a Cloud?—is in no doubt of the answer:

> I wield the flail of the lashing hail,
>   And whiten the green plains under,
> And then again I dissolve it in rain,
>   And laugh as I pass in thunder. . . .

The stars come like children round the moon:

> And I laugh to see them whirl and flee,
>   Like a swarm of golden bees. . . .

The mood is not reserved to the Cloud alone, for whom the rainbow is made as a triumphal arch:

> The sphere-fire above its soft colours wove,
>   While the moist Earth was laughing below.

And lastly, and here we may read a meaning that extends far beyond the life of a summer cloud, when the heavens are bare and ablaze as though the cloud had never been,—

> I silently laugh at my own cenotaph,
>   And out of the caverns of rain,
> Like a child from the womb, like a ghost from the tomb,
>   I arise and unbuild it again.

Next after *The Cloud* in Shelley's book comes an equally celebrated lyric, *To a Skylark*. The other day an old friend of mine whose powers of literary criticism have been subdued of late to his wonderful zest and originality in the novel and the play but will yet enrich us in the peace years, suddenly put his foot down, and declared that this poem was one of the worst ever written. I should wish then that a good many of us had the luck to write half as badly. But I have been wondering whether the verdict arose from a subconscious unwillingness to let Shelley ever make a joke or be, in his poems, on a sunshine holy day. For surely *To a Skylark* is another of the instances of his being somewhere outside the boundaries of complete gravity. He is, after all, talking to a bird whose abilities are light, airy, capricious, circling, all of a sudden, brilliant, and unpredictable. Catching the manner, the poet too becomes a flier into the sunshine, and professes to wish to have the secret, but he does not really want it; he will be in possession of it best by not deciding what it is, by letting it fly and sing unendingly. Hence all those questions, hence those similes flung up like the iris-touched spray of a fountain round the "sprite or bird." The poem is a game with an idea, a game that will never be lost or won. It is a song—and "must one swear to the truth of a song?" and yet a happy song, with heart-easing mirth like this, must ever be true as even ornithology can scarcely be. Or so I feel while Shelley, forgetting the Tories and his probable responsibility for the biggest estates in Sussex, sees and hears the lark

in an entertainment which has not yet dropped into
the darkness.

In some ways the saddest of Shelley's personal poems,
however a conversational gesture disguises it, is one addressed to Mary Shelley, who had—she even!—found "no
human interest" in his *Witch of Atlas*. She who had written
Frankenstein was dissatisfied that there was "no story." So,
in his very life, Shelley was confronted with the realisation
that an author's intention can be quite missed when a
reader's desires do not jump with it. But he was deeper
struck than most authors are upon this prevalent misfortune,
or he would not have exclaimed:

> O let me not believe
> That anything of mine is fit to live!

Still, most authors do not offer a creation so magical as his
Witch to the public. He was the boy Shelley when he
devised this beautiful doll—devised and dressed and got her
working in three astonishing days. She was a modern doll
too, for she was electrical. But Shelley on electricity is quit.
beyond any of our clever boys. He would have pleased them,
sure enough, at Christmas parties, but we have scarcely lived
up to his exhilaration in the power behind the illumina-
tions. "Men scarcely know how beautiful fire is," he says
in this same poem, and this rarest fire must still be given
the glory of his words while we pay the quarterly account
for its humble duty:

> And it unfurled its heaven-coloured pinions,
>   With stars of fire spotting the stream below;
> And from above into the Sun's dominions
>   Flinging a glory, like the golden glow
> In which Spring clothes her emerald-winged minions,
>   All interwoven with fine feathery snow
> And moonlight splendour of intensest rime,
> With which frost paints the pines in winter time.

But this is only one of the multitude of inventions with which Shelley costumed his Witch—the boy, the classic, the scientist, the reformer, the poet all united in a three days' jollification which still contains much for deep discussion. It will only lead to that if it be first enjoyed.

Out of all the rest that seems to be written by Ariel in conjunction with our poets, I must content myself with but one poet's work—a poet, of whom it is customary to speak as Chaucer speaks of the son of Morpheus, "he slept, and did no other work." But Coleridge would have answered in his own words, "My eyes make pictures when they are shut." He is still the musician *par excellence* among our poets, and in that quality lies something of his secret of making his profoundest thoughts and feelings easy to us. His *Ancient Mariner*, who continues to rule the waves, is "easy." The invention is "just a little thing"—there is a wedding, and one of the guests is held up by an old fellow with a yarn about a Ship. He is not pleased about it, especially when he hears the music over the way—the bassoon—perhaps he was himself a bit of a bassoonist. And can the grandest poetry, the most naked exposition of the soul and conscience, be so approached, much as if we were wandering into the Greyhounds? That is where Coleridge answers with the fact. Before very long, and still with a courtesy of spirit, the Mariner has the Guest, and that is Everyman, with him in the seas where the shadows are crimson, and the soul has a thirst as a tongue heaped with dust, and—back to the glorious day where life beloved really matters. Here *is* a story, and the flesh bows down before it, to hear—

> A noise as of a hidden brook
> In the leafy month of June.

Here accordingly I think I perceive that sovran humour which so freshens and endears our English poetry even when it most strenuously wrestles with the eternal perplexities: I perceive it not least in the fact that the Guest, cheated of his champagne so to speak, feels sadder next morning.

There is a much later poem by S. T. C. which in another tune announces him as enjoying delight with liberty and giving us the benefit. He was growing old, and the contrast between his invalid state and the high spirits which were his, as it seemed, only yesterday occurred to him as a subject for poetry. In the result we have a sad but a sweet music, and *Youth and Age* is its name; but youth wins, and you do not think as you read it of a corpulent old man with snuff on his waistcoat and the burden of the age of Napoleon on his shoulders, but of all that "ever was joyous, and fresh, and clear." He escapes out of time and we know what it was that made him so much of a portent in youth up and down England—such, that a desire to supply him with an income just to go on being Coleridge was expressed by some, and even put into action:

> Verse, a breeze mid blossoms straying,
> Where Hope clung feeding like a bee—
> Both were mine! Life went a-maying
>   With Nature, Hope, and Poesy,
>   When I was young!
> When I was young!

But the hesitation does not end the matter:

> I see these locks in silvery slips,
> This drooping gait, this altered size:
> But springtime blossoms on thy lips,
> And tears take sunshine from thine eyes!
> Life is but thought: so think I will
> That Youth and I are house-mates still.

May this not be called the pure poetry of sport and play?

If the English poets sometimes grit their teeth, find their biggest folio blank-books, and determine to compose a stupendous and exalted work, "the highest production of the human mind," it appears that they do not invariably get where they meant. The *Festus* of Philip James Bailey is lying stranded somewhere on the reefs of time, and no one bothers; the *Polyolbion* of Drayton, though we applaud him for desiring to see England first, is stacked away behind the lost property; and the *Idylls of the King* do not count for righteousness so much as sycophancy to Tennyson, whose *Northern Farmer*, even if not locally faultless, is still bustling along without benefit of any one except the humorous genius. We are properly suspicious of official poetry, and when we are asked to attend to epics designed to supply "a want" of epics, we retire as Dr. Johnson did from Thomson on *Liberty*. "Recoil" I think was his word; but the theme forbids me to press for academic niceties.

These ruminations may be impugned as far too devious from the due course of the book; but I am prepared to argue their consonance with all the rest. For one thing, I can ever feel that the game which made me write at all is not terminated at the boundary, but is reflected beyond, is echoed and varied out there among the gardens and the barns, the dells and the thickets, and belongs to some wider field. For another, I could even associate Shelley with the game; for, as we have seen, when writing in one of his metaphysical enthusiasms, he has to illustrate roundness—what else at once presents itself to him as *the* illustration but a cricket ball? But, predominantly and finally, these our poets and their lovely way of giving the serious things the air of free play and pastime are brothers of the man who, in all our entrenchments under bombardment, still comes out with a genius for throwing a light and hue of blessing, and fun, and golden days and dancing hopes, and "a grace without a name" over whatever the fiends may scrawl on the mists.

XXIII

All That Summer Glory

I AM content to leave the matter there, and, to speak more seriously, I do not grieve beyond endurance if the game of which I have been a follower so long is to be superseded and overshadowed one of these days. Of the immense good which it has done, the virtue which it has instilled or improved, the refreshment and intelligent diversion and pleasure and day-dream which it has brought some centuries of people, I have no doubt at all. It has proved itself the masterpiece of British games invention, and the competitors of its youth are long since only picturesque occasionals or glossary games:

> all exploytes a man can thinke or speake;
> As shove-groate, venter-poynte, or crosse the pile,
> As "beshrow him that's last at yonder stile,"
> As leapynge ore a Midsommer bon-fier,
> Or at the drawing Dun out of the myer;
> At "shoote-cock, Gregory," stool-ball, and what not,
> Pickle-point, tappe and scourge, to make him hott.

With one or two other games, it has been the support of that charming and merry and exciting tradition, not I think exampled in other kingdoms, of village team going forth to meet village team. If all this and so much more come to an end, and the course of human outlook and desire pass beyond this particular meadow, why must we lament for the future? "All sinks to re-ascend" in another form. There will be sport and pastime, there may be finer and richer recreation than ever. Travel has not yet come to its maturity. That is only one of the entrancing possibilities.

The determined cricketer, the last-ditch defender of "a man's game," is known to say loud and improper things against the god of Love, whose wings it seems can still carry off many a promising player from the season's "fixtures." After all, this god is elder than most. There is not much risk of *his* green fields becoming deserted; and his pastime is little altered since the happy Garden. The only thing that may be bettered in his triumphant lists is the touch of rude haste observable there too in the upheaval which we are going through. But that golden head was not meant for such harum-scarum chase, and when the times come and philosophy obtains the lasting victory will reappear in the older light. I have been noticing the statutes of the Court of Love, in a poem written by an imitator of Chaucer—twenty at least, and some might not be often obeyed even in the bannered halls of yesterday; for instance (to give the law in old rhyme but not spelling):

> The XIX. Statute. Meat and drink forget,
> Each other day see that thou fast for love,
> For in the Court they live withouten meat,
> Save such as cometh from Venus all above;
> Take they no heed, in pain of great reprove,
> Of meat and drink; for that is all in vain.
> Only they live by sight of their Sovereign.

Without the enforcement of this diet, Love in the future might yet regain much if the spirit of such ideals is understood. That, however, is for the discernment of the Benedicks and Beatrices who are still to come to love-matches, and when it shall be said once more of Mars by Venus:

> Over my altars hath he hung his lance,
> His batter'd shield, his uncontrolled crest,
> And for my sake, hath learn'd to sport and dance,
> To toy, to wanton, dally, smile and jest,
> Scorning his churlish drum and ensign red,
> Making my arms his field, his tent my bed.

Thus he that overruled I oversway'd,
Leading him prisoner in a red-rose chain.

Much besides the Love that Shakespeare sung, and Burns, may be rediscovered when the world grows young again at last; the order of Othello has only to go forth for the freshened breezes of "delight with liberty" to charm away to the green and the woodland and waterfall beyond the green. Then, whether it is still the reign of cricket or—forgive it, cricketer—some other noble pastime have arisen, there will be a myriad meanings in the word recreation, and each being will find his own and find it the best. Were I to start out on life again, and to stay until the times belong once more to the loves and graces, I do not believe that I should "make one" so long on the cricket ground as the early circumstances of my present allotted span so easily taught me to do. Would it not be the happiest game of all to be one of the wanderers who have made up the numbers of the British water-colour school, to rove away from time to time and capture the loveliest scenes in city and in upland, to bring home for the pleasure of the least sophisticated and the least explorative as well as the most a harvest of such simple beauties? To find the world a playground such as it must have been to J. M. W. Turner would be the chance of one such in a few centuries, yet I think we might all aspire to some friendship with the gentle art in which William Callow was so pleasant a coach, so pretty a craftsman for almost a century. But then, as he says, he never met with cricket and its companion manly sports when he was a boy. He missed the Second Eleven, the Heytesbury Estate C.C., Rupert's squadron of publisher-cricketers, and—the Paladins. I do not see how I could give them up; but there are ingenious Paladins who do get the best of both, or of more worlds. John H. who plays cricket with the glory of an Elizabethan making for the Spice Islands—he has been there—is no mean artist. Moreover, as long as Cordelia and I may lose ourselves in the enjoyment of the cottages and castles, the snowy mornings and the moonrises, the reapers and the resting cattle, the mountain ranges and the cathedral labyrinths of the artists, we shall count it our pastime as much as theirs.

But I was forgetting. Those who write, no matter what is decided among the observers of their contributions, have given their lives to one of the greatest sports of all. It is certainly a recreation and not a relaxation. It may be that experience in writing as in other recreation is a great advantage, but for my part I can never start out once more into the field of expression without the sense that this new innings is as difficult and as exacting as any that I ever tried. There is no duplication of conditions, and what was proved to be the natural and necessary way last week has to be resisted or at any rate reconsidered now that another set of facts and fancies and impressions challenges the player of words and phrases. Possibly as he grows older his apprehension of the odds against his essential success, his dissatisfaction with what he makes of the contest, grows more acute. The very greatest authors have spoken a little sadly on this severe nature of the game of experience and communication which they adorn with their achievements.

In a letter dated 8 Plains of Waterloo, Ramsgate, October 10th 1825, Samuel Taylor Coleridge looks into this endless disputation. "My Dear Friend," he opens, "it is a flat'ning thought that the more we have seen, the less we have to say." He represents the Mind and Nature as they appear in a literary man's early life under the figure of "two rival artists both potent magicians. . . . each having for its object to turn the other into canvas to paint on, clay to mould, or cabinet to contain." He goes on—and being Coleridge, he *does* go on:

"for a while the mind seems to have the better in the contest, and makes of Nature what it likes, takes her lichens and weather-stains for types and printers' ink, and prints maps and facsimiles of Arabic and Sanscrit MSS. on her rocks; composes country dances on her moonshiny ripples, fandangos on her waves, and waltzes on her eddy-pools, transforms her summer gales into harps and harpers, lovers' sighs and sighing lovers, and her winter blasts into Pindaric Odes, Christabels, and Ancient Mariners set to music by Beethoven, and in the insolence of triumph conjures her clouds into whales and walruses with palanquins on their backs, and chases the dodging stars in a sky-hunt! But alas! alas! that Nature is a wary, wily, long-breathed old witch, tough-lived as a turtle and divisible as the polyp, repullulative in a thousand snips and cuttings, *integra et in toto*. She is sure to get the better of Lady *Mind* in the long run and to take her revenge too; transforms our to-day into a canvas dead-coloured to receive the dull, featureless portrait of yesterday: not alone turns the mimic mind, the ci-devant sculptress with all her kaleidoscopic freaks and symmetries! into clay, but *leaves* it such a *clay* to cast dumps or bullets in. . . . Finis! and what is all this about? Why, verily, my dear friend! the thought forced itself on me, as I was beginning to put down the first sentence of this letter, how impossible it would have been fifteen or even ten years ago for me to have travelled and voyaged by land, river, and sea a hundred and twenty miles with fire and water blending their souls for my propulsion, as if I had been riding on a centaur with a sopha for a saddle, and yet to have nothing more to tell of it than that we had a very fine day and ran aside the steps in Ramsgate Pier at half-past four exactly. . . ."

When we find Coleridge, the heaven-eyed, the eloquent, looking round the field in this mood, and confessing that he after all his seasons of prowess is not too comfortable, and that each new occasion is newly exacting, then we others in the lower strata of his Mind and Nature match may fairly claim forgiveness for similar feelings. It is always the same story. There within our sense, joyous at setting forth, we thought we had such worlds to conquer, and there is little doubt that they were, and are, the settings of our adventure. But the opposition within ourselves and in the nature of existence is rather more severe than we foretold. It was easier, or it looked easier, until we stepped to the deed in this changeable light, and veering wind, and crumbling pitch, and encirclement of disturbing intentions, and inadequate resource, and slowly weakening powers of body. Then, where is that word "simple" in one's vocabulary? So it must be granted by one who, as I now have done, endeavours to set down in words the prodigality and the subtlety of an aspect of life which shone so wonderfully at so many an instant, and which went its way. The innings of the written record will not be what we dreamed. Can all that summer glory have left no more to us than this? But it is in the attempt that the justification may be found; the loser may have his victory; it was after all—a little luck there, a stern battle there, in the sun or the foul light, going slow or flashing past—a glorious game.

THE END